REVISE BTEC TECH AWARD

Health and Social Care

PRACTICE ASSESSMENTS Plus+

Series Consultant: Harry Smith
Author: Elizabeth Haworth

A note from the publisher

These practice assessments are designed to complement your revision and to help prepare you for the external assessment. They do not include all the content and skills needed for the complete course and have been written to help you practise what you have learned. They may not be representative of a real assessment.

While the publishers have made every attempt to ensure that advice on the qualification and its assessment is accurate, the official specification and associated assessment guidance materials are the only authoritative source of information and should always be referred to for definitive guidance.

This qualification is reviewed on a regular basis and may be updated in the future. Any such updates that affect the content of this book will be outlined at www.pearsonfe.co.uk/BTECchanges.

Published by Pearson Education Limited, 80 Strand, London, WC2R ORL.
www.pearsonschoolsandfecolleges.co.uk

Copies of official specifications for all Pearson qualifications may be found on the website: qualifications.pearson.com

Typeset, produced and illustrated by QBS Learning Ltd
Cover illustration by Miriam Sturdee

The right of Elizabeth Haworth to be identified as author of this work has been asserted by her in accordance with the Copyright, Designs and Patents Act 1988.

First published 2019
22 21 20 19
10 9 8 7 6 5 4 3 2 1

British Library Cataloguing in Publication Data
A catalogue record for this book is available from the British Library

ISBN 978 1 292 30699 5

Acknowledgements
5, 19, 48: Blood Pressure Association: www.bloodpressureuk.org/BloodPressu-reandyou/Thebasics/Bloodpressurechart. Used with permission; **20, 34:** Häggström, M (2014). 'Medical gallery of Mikael Häggström 2014'. *WikiJournal of Medicine 1* (2). DOI:10.15347/wjm/2014.008. ISSN 2002-4436. Content licensed under the Creative Commons CC-0 licence; **20, 34:** Nunn, AJ and Gregg, I (1989). 'New regression equations for predicting peak expiratory flow in adults'. *British Medical Journal.* 298: 1068–1070. Adapted by Clement Clarke for use in EU scale. Peakflow.com – Predictive Normal Values (Nomogram, EU scale) Source data in tabulated form may be available from Clement Clarke International.

Printed in Slovakia by Neografia

Notes from the publisher

1. While the publishers have made every attempt to ensure that advice on the qualification and its assessment is accurate, the official specification and associated assessment guidance materials are the only authoritative source of information and should always be referred to for definitive guidance. Pearson examiners have not contributed to any sections in this resource relevant to examination papers for which they have responsibility.

2. Pearson has robust editorial processes, including answer and fact checks, to ensure the accuracy of the content in this publication, and every effort is made to ensure that this publication is free of errors. We are, however, only human, and occasionally errors do occur. Pearson is not liable for any misunderstandings that arise as a result of errors in this publication, but it is our priority to ensure that the content is accurate. If you spot an error, please do contact us at resourcescorrections@pearson.com so we can make sure that it is corrected.

Websites

Pearson Education Limited is not responsible for the content of any external internet sites. It is essential for tutors to preview each website before using it in class so as to ensure that the URL is still accurate, relevant and appropriate. We suggest that tutors bookmark useful websites and consider enabling learners to access them through the school/college intranet.

Introduction

This book has been designed to help you to practise the skills you may need for the external assessment of BTEC Tech Award **Health and Social Care**, Component 3: Health and Wellbeing.

About the practice assessments

The book contains four practice assessments for the component. Unlike your actual assessment, the questions have targeted hints, guidance and support in the margin to help you understand how to tackle them.

links to relevant pages in the Pearson Revise BTEC Tech Award Health and Social Care Revision Guide so you can revise the essential content. This will also help you to understand how the essential content is applied to different contexts when assessed.

to get you started and remind you of the skills or knowledge you need to apply.

to help you on how to approach a question, such as making a brief plan.

to provide content that you need to learn, such as a definition or principles related to health and social care.

to help you avoid common pitfalls.

to remind you of content related to the question to aid your revision on that topic.

for use with the final practice assessment to help you become familiar with answering in a given time and ways to think about allocating time for different questions.

There is space for you to write your answers to the questions within this book. However, if you require more space to complete your answers, you may want to use separate paper.

There is also an answer section at the back of the book, so you can check your answers for each practice assessment.

Check the Pearson website

For overarching guidance on the official assessment outcomes and key terms used in your assessment, please refer to the specification on the Pearson website.

The practice questions, support and answers in this book are provided to help you to revise the essential content in the specification, along with ways of applying your skills. Details of your actual assessment may change, so always make sure you are up to date on its format and requirements by asking your tutor or checking the Pearson website for the most up-to-date Sample Assessment Material, Mark Schemes and any past papers.

Contents

Practice assessment 1 1

Practice assessment 2 15

Practice assessment 3 30

Practice assessment 4 44

Answers 58

A small bit of small print

Pearson publishes Sample Assessment Material and the specification on its website. This is the official content and this book should be used in conjunction with it. The questions have been written to help you test your knowledge and skills. Remember: the real assessment may not look like this.

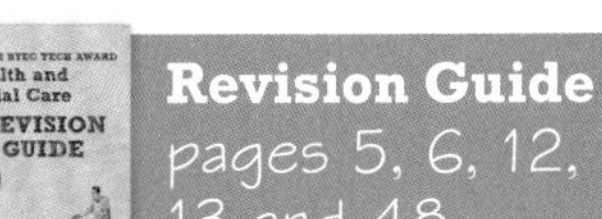

Practice assessment 1

You must complete ALL questions.

SECTION A: Assessing health and wellbeing

You are a health care assistant at Graston Health Centre. You have been asked to assess the health and wellbeing of one of the service users.

Read the information below and then complete the activities that follow.

Location
Suzie is 25 years old. She lives with her partner Dave, who is the same age, in a three-storey town house in the middle of a large town. The house has a small garden.

Medical history
Suzie has a tendency to worry about things and has occasional panic attacks. Her partner Dave travels all over the country for his job, so she eats on her own when he is away, often ordering takeaways or fast food. She also snacks, so her weight goes up and down. Suzie enjoys digging in their garden, getting satisfaction from growing her own flowers, while also exercising to help control her weight.

Family, friends and social interactions
Suzie and Dave live quite close to their families and friends, and socialise with them most weekends. They enjoy meals and drinks out or at home, and barbeques. Suzie finds that exercise distracts her from her worries and also helps to control her weight. When she has time, she attends exercise classes at the local gym. She sometimes goes for coffee afterwards with her friends from the gym.

Day-to-day life
Suzie is a teacher at a school 3 km from her home and, most evenings, brings home planning or marking to do. Dave has a stressful job that involves a lot of travelling and overnight stays in hotels. He is a successful salesman, so earns a lot of money based on how many sales he makes. The couple both enjoy their jobs and the lifestyle their income allows them.

Revision Guide pages 5, 6, 12, 13 and 48.

Hint

The assessment is divided into two sections. Section A is about **assessing health and wellbeing** and Section B is about **designing a health and wellbeing improvement plan**.

Prepare

Read this information carefully, underlining factors that affect Suzie's health and wellbeing, such as 'three-storey town house' and 'garden' in the **Location** section.

Hint

You will use the information in this scenario to help you answer the questions on pages 2–14.

Hint

Remember to reread this information each time you learn more about Suzie, as all the questions in this assessment are based on her life.

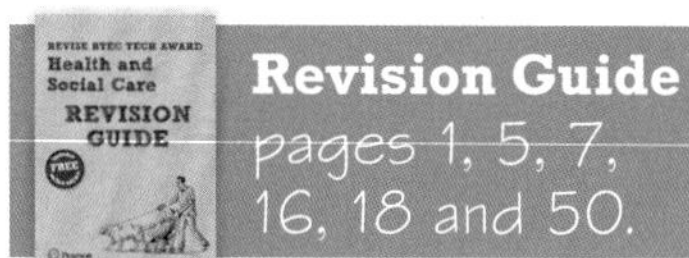

Revision Guide pages 1, 5, 7, 16, 18 and 50.

Hint

To **review** information, you need to consider the **facts** in the scenario. Identify any facts about Suzie's lifestyle that are likely to affect her health and wellbeing.

Hint

For **explain** questions like Questions 1(a) and 1(b), you need to identify a point from the information **and** then give further details to support your point.

LEARN IT!

Physical factors are ways in which Suzie's lifestyle affects her **body**.

Watch out!

In both Questions 1(a) and 1(b), you are being asked to explain factors that could have a **positive** effect. You will not get any marks if you write about negative effects.

LEARN IT!

Economic factors refer to how much money Suzie has.

Your manager at Graston Health Centre has asked you to review the information about Suzie.

1 (a) Explain **two physical** factors that could have a **positive** effect on Suzie's health and wellbeing.

Use the information provided.

1 ....

....

....

....

2 ....

....

....

....

4 marks

(b) Explain **one economic** factor that could have a **positive** effect on Suzie's health and wellbeing.

Use the information provided.

....

....

....

....

2 marks

(c) Explain **two social** factors that could have a **negative** effect on Suzie's health and wellbeing.

Use the information provided.

1 ....

....

....

....

2 ....

....

....

....

4 marks

(d) Explain **one emotional** factor that could have a **negative** effect on Suzie's health and wellbeing.

....

....

....

....

2 marks

Total for Question 1 = 12 marks

Revision Guide pages 1, 12, 13, 14, 49 and 51.

Hint

For Question 1(c), you should write about **two negative social factors** – two aspects of Suzie's lifestyle that stop her from interacting with other people.

Hint

In Question 1(c), make sure that you have identified **two** factors **and** have also added some **detail** about each of them. Remember that you are only being asked for examples of **negative** effects on Suzie's health and wellbeing.

Hint

For Question 1(d), to help you identify **one negative emotional factor**, go back to the scenario on page 1 and underline any words that relate to Suzie's emotional problems.

LEARN IT!

Emotional factors relate to positive and negative feelings. For example, **negative** feelings could be worry, sadness and stress.

Revision Guide
pages 1, 4, 12, 14, 16, 20 and 51.

Explore

Sepsis (blood poisoning) can result from bacterial infection and lead to organ failure.

Hint

From the scenario on page 1, you know that Suzie worries. For Question 2(a), consider how Dave's serious accident and life-threatening illness would make her **feel**.

Hint

An **impact** is an effect on a person or situation. Question 2(b) asks you to explain how looking after Dave has an **effect** on Suzie's social wellbeing. Impacts can be **positive** or **negative**.

Hint

Dave needs a lot of care, which will affect Suzie's social life. For Question 2(b), look back at the scenario on page 1 to remember what social activities Suzie did on her own and with Dave. Social activities include **work** and **leisure**.

Dave had a car accident while travelling for work and was admitted to hospital. He had several injuries, including a broken leg, and developed a severe infection in one of his wounds. He became extremely ill with sepsis, a life-threatening complication of infection. After being successfully treated in an intensive care unit, he returned home, having spent eight days in hospital. His doctors are hopeful that eventually he will make a full recovery, but he won't be able to return to work for at least eight weeks. While he still needs a lot of care, his mother is looking after him each day until Suzie gets home from work.

2 (a) Explain **two** effects that Dave's accident could have on Suzie's **emotional** wellbeing.

1 ....

....

....

....

2 ....

....

....

....

4 marks

(b) Explain **one** impact on Suzie's **social** wellbeing of having to look after Dave when she returns home from work and at the weekend.

....

....

....

....

2 marks

Total for Question 2 = 6 marks

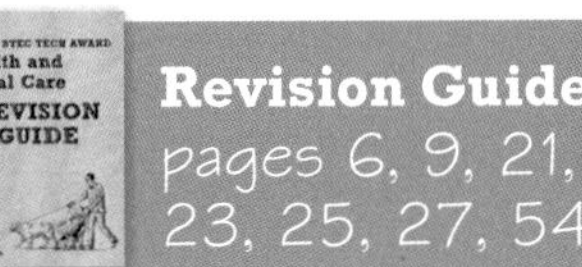

Revision Guide pages 6, 9, 21, 23, 25, 27, 54 and 56.

Lifestyle data

Suzie is worried about her weight, so has made an appointment to see Dr Martin, her general practitioner (GP).

Dr Martin asks Suzie some questions and records the following information:

- Suzie eats too many takeaways and snacks.
- Suzie binge drinks (drinks a lot of units of alcohol) at the weekend.
- Suzie is not able to attend her usual exercise class as she is caring for her partner, Dave.

Physiological data

Dr Martin records the following measurements.

Body mass index (BMI)	29.3 kg/m^2
Blood pressure	160/95 mm Hg

Guidance for physiological data

Dr Martin gives this guidance to help you interpret the physiological data.

BMI

Weight categories	**BMI (kg/m^2)**
Underweight	$<$18.5
Healthy weight	18.5–24.9
Overweight	25–29.9
Obese	30–34.9
Severely obese	35–39.9
Morbidly obese	$\geq$40

Blood pressure chart for adults

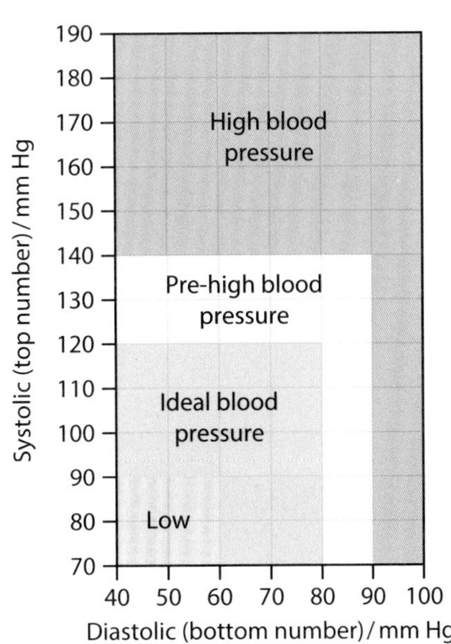

Hint

The key word **interpret** is asking you to work out what Suzie's physiological data say about her health.

Hint

To **interpret** Suzie's **BMI data**, find the table row that contains her BMI and read off her **weight category**. Consider how close her weight is to the next category.

Hint

To **interpret** Suzie's **blood pressure data**, find 160 on the vertical axis. Draw a line across from there. Find 95 on the horizontal axis. Draw a line up from there. Note the category in which the two lines meet.

Explore

High blood pressure is linked to stroke and heart attack. Consider the effects of a stroke or heart attack on someone like Suzie.

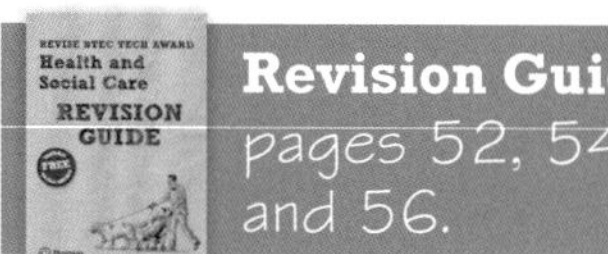

Revision Guide pages 52, 54 and 56.

Prepare

From the scenario information given so far, note down anything about Suzie's lifestyle that might affect her **BMI** and **blood pressure**.

Hint

You must **interpret** the data accurately, demonstrating this by correctly identifying Suzie's blood pressure and BMI/weight categories. Then show that you know about the implications for her health by clearly explaining the risks.

Hint

When writing about risks to Suzie's future health, you need to use **your own knowledge**. This information is not available in the scenario.

3 Explain what the data provided by Dr Martin suggest about:

- Suzie's current physical health
- risks to her future physical health.

Lifestyle data	**Suzie's current physical health:**
	....
	....
	....
	....
	Risks to Suzie's future physical health:
	....
	....
	....
	....
BMI	**Suzie's current physical health:**
	....
	....
	....
	....
	Risks to Suzie's future physical health:
	....
	....
	....
	....

Blood pressure	**Suzie's current physical health:**
	....
	Risks to Suzie's future physical health:
	....

Total for Question 3 = 12 marks

TOTAL FOR SECTION A = 30 MARKS

LEARN IT!

Remember that high blood pressure can lead to heart disease and heart attack, stroke, kidney disease and dementia. Low blood pressure causes dizziness but has less risk of long-term health problems.

Hint

Make sure you clearly state whether Suzie has high or low blood pressure, before explaining how this might be a risk to her current and future physical health.

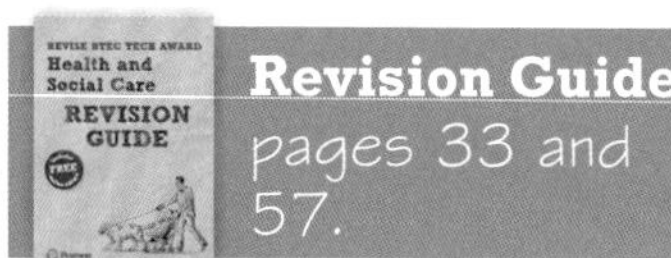

Revision Guide pages 33 and 57.

Hint

Remember to reread all the information provided in previous questions about Suzie's lifestyle, as well as thinking about this additional information.

Hint

Recall that Suzie often eats on her own during the week when Dave is away with work, and enjoys meals and drinks out at the weekend. Suzie will be better motivated to stick to your health and wellbeing improvement plan if she can reduce, rather than cut out, those aspects of her lifestyle that she enjoys and which help her to relax.

SECTION B: Designing a health and wellbeing improvement plan

You have been asked to design a health and wellbeing improvement plan for Suzie.

First you should look back at the information about Suzie from Questions 1, 2 and 3.

Then study the notes below, taken by Dr Martin.

Suzie wants to:

- find time to exercise
- eat a more balanced diet to lose weight
- reduce her stress
- drink less alcohol at weekends.

Suzie does not want to:

- cut out all meals with family and friends
- stop drinking alcohol altogether.

Other relevant information:

- Suzie is a highly motivated person once she puts her mind to a task.
- Suzie worries about getting her work done and finding enough time for exercise.
- Dave has recovered from his accident and is back to his normal work routine.

4 Design a health and wellbeing improvement plan for Suzie. Your plan should describe **three** recommended actions.

For each recommended action:

- set a short-term and a long-term target
- give **one** source of support
- explain how the source of support will help Suzie achieve the targets.

Recommended action 1
....
....
Short-term target
....
....
Long-term target
....
....
Source of support and how it will help
....
....

Revision Guide pages 5, 6, 7, 9, 14, 27, 28, 33, 34, 35, 36, 37, 38, 42, 43 and 58.

Hint

Recommended actions are things you suggest that Suzie can do to improve her health and wellbeing, and which take account of her situation.

Hint

The command word **describe** means you need to give a clear account of each action you are recommending for Suzie. To decide on actions that are suitable for Suzie, revisit Dr Martin's records on page 5.

Watch out!

You must identify sources of support **and** explain how each one helps achieve the target.

LEARN IT!

Make sure your targets are clear, realistic and helpful by ensuring they are **SMART**:

Specific – make your targets clear and exact

Measurable – explain how Suzie can measure and observe her progress

Achievable – ensure the target is possible for Suzie

Realistic – ensure the target is suitable for Suzie

Time-related – ensure you give a timeframe for both the short-term and long-term target so Suzie knows how long she has.

Revision Guide pages 5, 6, 7, 9, 14, 27, 28, 33, 34, 35, 36, 37, 38, 42, 43 and 58.

LEARN IT!

A **short-term target** is less than six months.

LEARN IT!

A **long-term target** is six months or more.

Hint

A source of support can be **formal** or **informal**. Both are acceptable. You could include examples of both to show that you understand that they are equally valuable.

Watch out!

Don't choose actions that are too similar. 'Eat more healthily' and 'Eat fewer restaurant meals' are both actions to do with diet. Include actions about different factors, such as alcohol intake and exercise.

Watch out!

Check how many marks are awarded for this question. Be sure to give sufficient **detail** under each heading to earn them all.

Recommended action 2 ....
Short-term target ....
Long-term target ....
Source of support and how it will help ....

Recommended action 3 ....
Short-term target ....
Long-term target ....
Source of support and how it will help ....

Total for Question 4 = 12 marks

5 Explain how your health improvement plan takes into account Suzie's needs, wishes and circumstances.

Revision Guide pages 29, 30, 31, 57 and 59.

Hint

Reread the information you have been given about Suzie throughout this assessment paper, making sure you use **all** of the information.

Prepare

For a long-answer question like Question 5, you could make a brief **writing plan**. You could include a paragraph on each of your three recommended actions, showing how you have taken into account Suzie's **needs**, **wishes** and **circumstances**. Then add a short conclusion to justify your health and wellbeing improvement plan.

Watch out!

You must only refer to facts you have been given when answering this question. **Do not** invent other factors or make assumptions about Suzie.

Hint

Show that you have adopted a **person-centred approach** by taking into account Suzie's needs, wishes and circumstances on page 8, and by referring to other relevant information from the scenario. For example, Suzie **needs** to lose weight but **wishes** to continue eating with family and friends at the weekend. One of her **circumstances** is that she often eats alone now Dave is back at work after a serious accident.

Hint

Check your **spelling**, **punctuation** and **grammar**. It will help the assessor to better understand your answer if it is easy to read.

Total for Question 5 = 10 marks

6 Describe possible obstacles that Suzie may experience when trying to follow your health and wellbeing improvement plan, and suggest how these could be reduced or overcome.

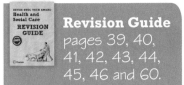

Revision Guide pages 39, 40, 41, 42, 43, 44, 45, 46 and 60.

Hint

For Question 6, a **describe** question, give an account of each obstacle and say how it can be overcome.

Make a **writing plan**. Include a paragraph for each obstacle, stating the problem and giving realistic suggestions for how it can be minimised. Give a brief conclusion, justifying your suggestions.

Watch out!

Make realistic suggestions. For example, it is **not** realistic to relieve Suzie's stress by suggesting she doesn't do any marking or preparation. She is a teacher and these are essential parts of her job. It **is** realistic to suggest she stays at school to do it, so when she gets home she can relax.

Hint

The word **possible** in Question 6 means you can use **your own wider knowledge** of health and wellbeing, rather than just the facts about Suzie's lifestyle provided in the scenario.

Hint

Check that your answer is clear, your points are easy to understand and that you have answered the question. If not, make some changes to your answer now.

Prepare

Aim to use the **PEEL approach** in a long answer. Each paragraph should follow this format:

Point: make one point

Explain: explain this point

Evidence: justify (give reasons to support) the point and explanation

Link: link back to the question.

Try this approach when you are answering Questions 5 and 6.

Total for Question 6 = 8 marks

TOTAL FOR SECTION B = 30 MARKS **TOTAL FOR TASK = 60 MARKS**

Practice assessment 2

You must complete ALL questions.

SECTION A: Assessing health and wellbeing

You are a health care assistant at Brookmill Surgery. You have been asked to assess the health and wellbeing of one of the service users.

Read the information below and then complete the activities that follow.

Location
Muhammad is 55 years old. He and his wife Aamal are patients at Brookmill Surgery. They live in a large detached house with a big garden, located in a village and surrounded by countryside.

Medical history
Muhammad has a stressful job and, because he smokes, he is prone to chest infections.

Family, friends and social interactions
Muhammad and Aamal have two grown-up children and four grandchildren, who live some distance away in other parts of the country. The couple usually see their family in the school holidays. They have lots of friends in the village and at the golf club, where they are both members.

Day-to-day life
Muhammad and Aamal are both accountants. For most of their working day, they sit at their computers or in meetings. They enjoy their jobs and the lifestyle their incomes allow, which includes regular meals out with their friends at local restaurants or at home, playing rounds of golf and socialising at the golf club.
Muhammad and Aamal's faith is important to them – they pray several times a day and Aamal chooses to wear a hijab (headscarf) – but they live too far away from a mosque to attend very often. They don't drink alcohol. They are the only Muslims in their village and they have been abused online about their faith and culture.

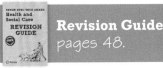

Revision Guide pages 48.

Hint

Questions have **command words** (for example **assess**, **explain** and **describe**) that tell you what to do. Your teacher will explain how to respond to these words.

Hint

The command word here is **assess**, meaning to consider the information and reach a judgement or conclusion.

Explore

As in all religions, some Muslims are **devout**, closely observing the faith's teachings and practices, while others are less deeply committed. Muslims follow the religion of **Islam**, based on the teachings of the prophet Muhammad, and worship one God, Allah. Prayer, charity, fasting and pilgrimage are important to practising Muslims.

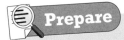

Prepare

Remember **CUBE**:

Circle the command verb.

Underline key information in the question.

Box key information in the case study.

Ensure you read the question at least twice.

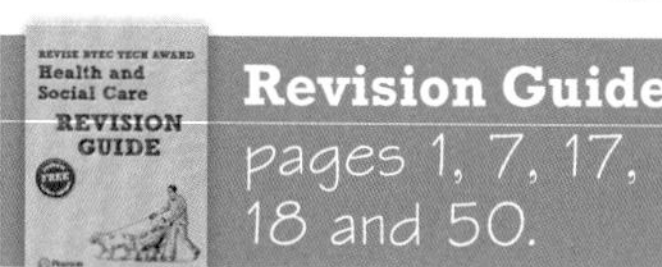

Revision Guide pages 1, 7, 17, 18 and 50.

Hint

To **review** the information, look back at the scenario to identity any factors that could affect Muhammad's health and wellbeing.

Hint

The command word in Questions 1(a) and 1(b) is **explain**. This means you need to identify factors with a **positive** effect on Muhammad's health and wellbeing **and then** give further details to support your point.

LEARN IT!

Environmental factors relate to the space we live in, including location, living conditions and the purity of the surrounding air, water and land. **Physical factors** relate to body systems and include diet and exercise.

Watch out!

Environmental factors can be closely related to physical factors. Do **not** use an answer for Question 1(b) that you used in Question 1(a).

The Practice Manager at Brookmill Surgery has asked you to review the information about Muhammad.

1 (a) Explain **two environmental** factors that could have a **positive** effect on Muhammad's health and wellbeing.

Use the information provided.

1 ....

....

....

....

2 ....

....

....

....

4 marks

(b) Explain **one physical** factor that could have a **positive** effect on Muhammad's health and wellbeing.

Use the information provided.

....

....

....

....

2 marks

(c) Explain **two emotional** factors that could have a **negative** effect on Muhammad's health and wellbeing.

Use the information provided.

1 ....

....

....

....

2 ....

....

....

....

4 marks

(d) Explain **one cultural** factor that could have a **negative** effect on Muhammad's health and wellbeing.

....

....

....

....

2 marks

Total for Question 1 = 12 marks

Revision Guide pages 1, 12, 13, 14, 49 and 51.

Hint

For Question 1(c), an **explain** question, **identify two** factors from the scenario and **expand on each one** to provide a clear explanation of how it has a negative effect on Muhammad's health and wellbeing.

Hint

For Question 1(c), don't forget that **emotional** factors can affect physical, intellectual and social wellbeing. Thinking in a joined-up way can lead to better answers.

Prepare

Refer back to the scenario on page 15 to identify **negative** factors.

Cultural factors relate to areas such as the arts, language, religion, cuisine and social habits of particular groups of people.

Watch out!

If you use an emotional factor that relates to Muhammad's culture to answer Question 1(c), be sure to make a different point in Question 1(d).

Revision Guide pages 1, 14, 16 and 20.

Prepare

To answer Question 2(a), reread the scenario on page 15 and consider the facts provided here. You could draw on information about Muhammad's work, how he likes to relax, his social life and where his children live, for example.

Hint

For **explain** questions such as Questions 2(a) or 2(b), state the **effect** or **impact** and **expand** on your point by linking to what you know about Muhammad from the scenario.

Hint

An **impact** can be **positive** or **negative**.

Explore

A stroke is life-threatening. Blood supply in the brain is interrupted by a clot or a bleed, often leading to paralysis and loss of speech. Think about how Aamal's stroke could affect the couple's lifestyle.

Aamal has had a stroke and, after months in hospital, is finally well enough to be allowed home. She has temporarily lost the use of her left leg and arm, so is using a wheelchair. Muhammad is taking time off work to drive Aamal to regular physiotherapy sessions at the hospital. Her consultant is hopeful that she will eventually recover most of her mobility. At the moment, Aamal needs help with washing, dressing, toileting and eating, so she has visits from home-support services during the day while Muhammad is at work. Once he is home, he takes over her care.

2 (a) Explain **two** effects of Aamal's stroke on Muhammad's **social** wellbeing.

1 ....

....

....

....

2 ....

....

....

....

4 marks

(b) Explain **one** impact of Aamal's home-support services on Muhammad's **emotional** wellbeing.

....

....

....

....

2 marks

Total for Question 2 = 6 marks

Lifestyle data

Muhammad attends Brookmill Surgery for a health check. Dr Wilson, his general practitioner (GP), asks some questions and finds out the following information:

- Muhammad does not eat a healthy diet.
- Muhammad smokes at least 40 cigarettes a day.

Physiological data

Dr Wilson records the following measurements.

Height	190 cm
Blood pressure	170/100 mm Hg
Peak flow	466 l/min

Guidance for physiological data

Dr Wilson gives this guidance to help you interpret the physiological data.

Blood pressure chart for adults

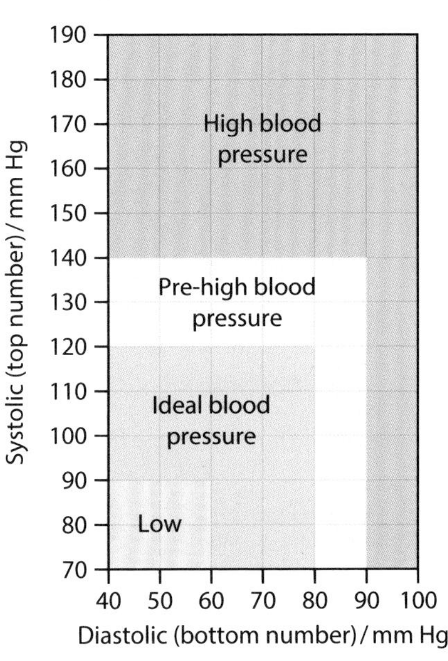

Revision Guide pages 6, 10, 23, 24, 26, 54 and 55.

Prepare

You should be familiar with **physiological indicators** such as blood pressure and peak flow. Consider what this new information tells you about Muhammad's current health and any risks to his future health.

Hint

In order to **interpret** the data, you need to be able to understand and state the meaning of the readings given.

Hint

To **interpret** the data about Muhammad's **blood pressure**, mark where the systolic value (170 mm Hg) meets the diastolic value (100 mm Hg) and read off the category.

Hint

To **interpret** the data about Muhammad's **peak flow**, find his age on the horizontal axis. Follow the vertical line up until it meets the curve for men of his height. His expected peak flow is shown on the vertical axis level where the vertical line meets the curve. Compare with his actual peak flow.

Explore

Consider the short- and long-term effects of smoking, eating an unhealthy diet, not getting enough exercise and being under stress.

continued...

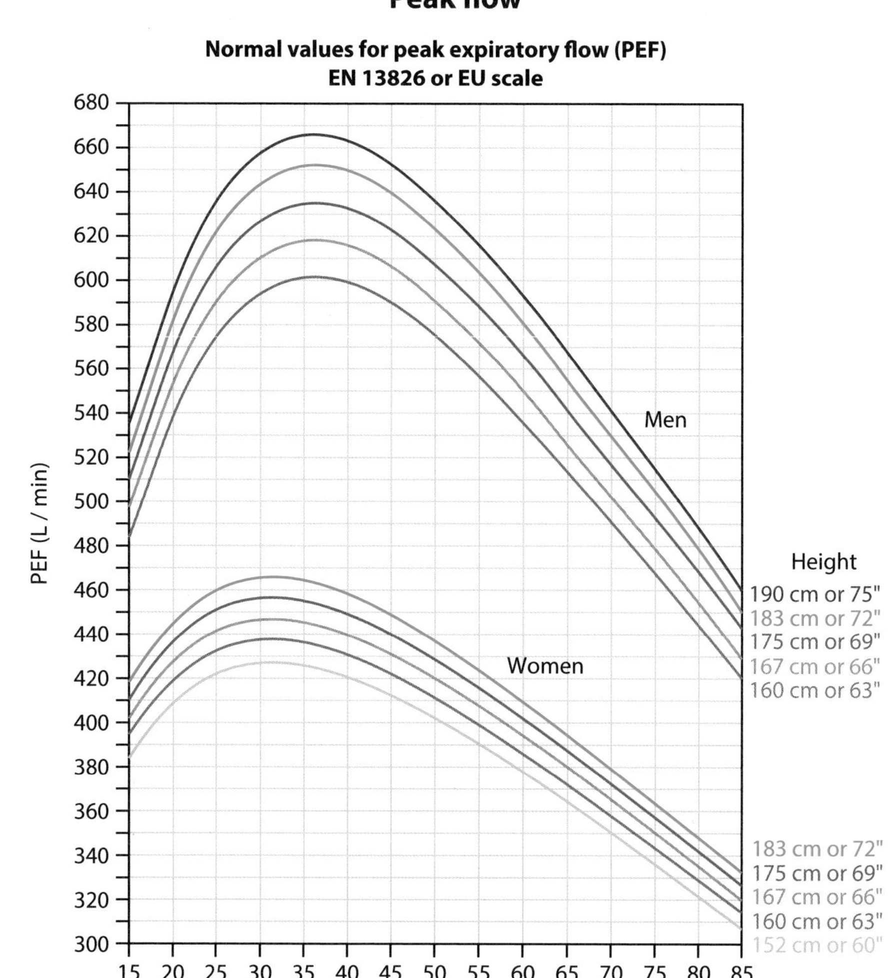

3 Explain what the data provided by Dr Wilson suggest about:

- Muhammad's current physical health
- risks to his future physical health.

Lifestyle data	**Muhammad's current physical health:**
	....
	....
	....
	....
	Risks to Muhammad's future physical health:
	....
	....
	....
	....
Blood pressure	**Muhammad's current physical health:**
	....
	....
	....
	....
	Risks to Muhammad's future physical health:
	....
	....
	....
	....

Revision Guide pages 52, 54 and 56.

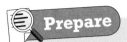

Prepare

Consider Muhammad's lifestyle data and reread all the information presented so far. Note aspects of Muhammad's lifestyle that could affect his blood pressure and peak flow.

Hint

Low peak flow indicates poor lung function. **High blood pressure** shows that the cardiovascular system is straining. You need to know what causes low peak flow and high blood pressure, then link your knowledge to information about Muhammad.

Hint

The number of lines gives an idea of how many points to make.

Explore

Recall what you know about **short-term** and **long-term effects** of smoking, eating an unhealthy diet, not exercising enough and being under stress. Short-term effects are usually minor physical symptoms, but long-term effects include risk of serious diseases.

Peak flow	**Muhammad's current physical health:**
	....
	....
	....
	....
	Risks to Muhammad's future physical health:
	....
	....
	....
	....

Total for Question 3 = 12 marks

TOTAL FOR SECTION A = 30 MARKS

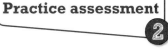

SECTION B: Designing a health and wellbeing improvement plan

ou have been asked to design a health and wellbeing improvement plan r Muhammad.

irst you should look back at the information about Muhammad from uestions 1, 2 and 3.

hen study the notes below, taken by Dr Wilson.

Muhammad wants to:
- get more exercise
- eat a more balanced diet
- stop smoking
- reduce his stress levels.

Muhammad does **not** want to:
- cut out all meals with friends
- stop playing golf, even though he finds it hard to fit in with looking after Aamal.

Other relevant information:
- Muhammad is a highly motivated person.
- Muhammad thinks he should have noticed that Aamal was working too hard and feels guilty about her stroke.

Revision Guide pages 29, 33 and 57.

Prepare

Remember to use any other relevant information provided so far about Muhammad's lifestyle, as well as this additional information. You could make notes on this page.

Hint

This part of the scenario describes Muhammad's **needs**, **wants** and **circumstances**. Circumstances are given in the bullet points under **Other relevant information**. You should take these three aspects into account for a **person-centred approach** to designing your plan.

Hint

If a person is **highly motivated**, they are driven to succeed. So, once Muhammad has made up his mind to stick to a health and wellbeing improvement plan, he is likely to see it through to the end.

Revision Guide

pages 6, 7, 10, 26, 28, 34, 35, 36, 37, 38, 43 and 58.

Hint

The command word in Question 4 is **describe**, so you need to give a clear account of each action you are recommending. Link this to the information about Muhammad which is provided in the scenario.

Hint

A **recommended action** is a suggestion for Muhammad to follow, in order to improve his health and wellbeing.

LEARN IT!

A **target** is an identified and achievable step towards Muhammad's overall goal.

LEARN IT!

Make sure your targets are clear, realistic and helpful by ensuring they are **SMART**: Specific, Measurable, Achievable, Realistic and Time-related.

Hint

Another key word in Question 4 is **give**, which means you have to state a source of support. You also need to **explain** how it will help Muhammad, so you should add some detail.

4 Design a health and wellbeing improvement plan for Muhammad. Your plan should describe **three** recommended actions.

For each recommended action:

- set a short-term and a long-term target
- give **one** source of support
- explain how the source of support will help Muhammad achieve the targets.

Recommended action 1
....
Short-term target   ....
Long-term target   ....
Source of support and how it will help   ....

Recommended action 2

....

....

Short-term target

....

....

Long-term target

....

....

Source of support and how it will help

....

....

Recommended action 3

....

....

Short-term target

....

....

Long-term target

....

....

Source of support and how it will help

....

....

Total for Question 4 = 12 marks

Revision Guide pages 6, 7, 10, 26, 28, 34, 35, 36, 37, 38, 43 and 58.

Prepare

To design Muhammad's health and wellbeing improvement plan, refer back to the information you learned about him earlier in the assessment.

LEARN IT!

Examples of **formal** support: health care professionals and voluntary organisations. Examples of **informal** support: family, friends and work colleagues.

Watch out!

Only **one** answer is required in the first three rows of the Recommended action boxes, but **two** answers are needed in the last row. Here you should identify a source of support **and** say how it could help Muhammad.

Watch out!

Avoid recommending actions that focus on the same factor. The factors that concern Muhammad are diet, exercise, smoking and stress.

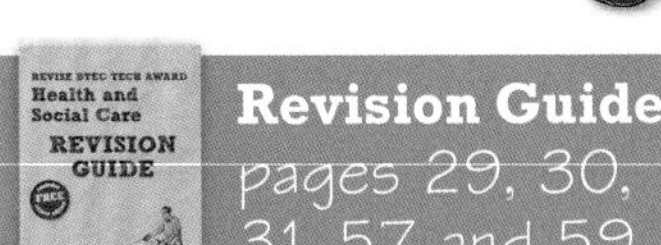

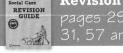

Revision Guide pages 29, 30, 31, 57 and 59.

Hint

For information about Muhammad's **needs, wishes** and **circumstances**, refer to page 23. Be sure to cover all three aspects.

Hint

In Question 5, **'takes into account'** means that you have **considered** Muhammad's needs, wishes and circumstances when designing your health and wellbeing improvement plan.

Hint

To **explain** your improvement plan, you should provide a **rationale** (reasons) that shows how it is suitable for Muhammad.

Prepare

Make a brief writing plan before you write a longer answer. Each paragraph should use the PEEL format: Make one **Point**, **Explain** this point, use **Evidence** to justify the point and explanation, and **Link** back to the question.

Try this when you are answering Questions 5 and 6.

5 Explain how your health improvement plan takes into account Muhammad's needs, wishes and circumstances.

Revision Guide pages 29, 30, 31, 57 and 59.

Hint

Be led by the space provided when deciding how much detail to give in your answer.

Hint

Question 5 requires you to **justify** your health and wellbeing improvement plan. Give valid reasons for your recommendations and support these with **evidence** about Muhammad which is drawn from the whole scenario. For example, you could say that he might aim to play golf twice a week to ensure he gets the exercise.

Hint

Read through your answer to check it makes sense. Accurate spelling, punctuation and grammar will make your answer easier to read and understand.

Hint

Double check that your improvement plan fits with the facts in the scenario so far, especially with Muhammad's needs, wishes and circumstances.

Total for Question 5 = 10 marks

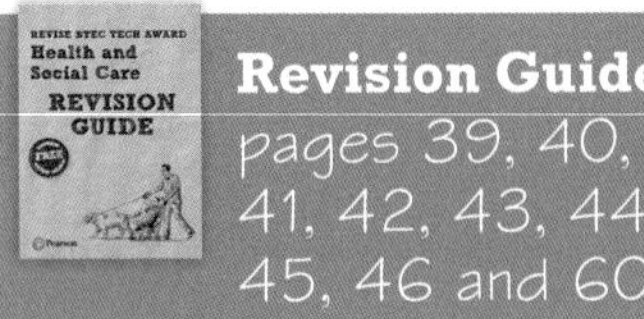

Revision Guide pages 39, 40, 41, 42, 43, 44, 45, 46 and 60.

Hint

Obstacles are difficulties which Muhammad might face when following your health and wellbeing improvement plan. It is important to reduce or overcome obstacles that may hinder Muhammad's progress.

Hint

Question 6 is a **describe** question. You need to give an account of each obstacle **and** suggestions for addressing them. For example, Aamal's hospital appointments may be during his work time, so he could talk to his boss about working flexible hours.

Watch out!

Question 6 asks about **possible** obstacles. So, you have to think of problems that could happen using information from the **scenario and your own wider knowledge**. For example, Muhammad has caring responsibilities, so may be short of time.

Watch out!

Your suggestions for overcoming barriers need to be **realistic** – sensible, suitable and achievable – for Muhammad.

6 Describe possible obstacles that Muhammad may experience when trying to follow your health and wellbeing improvement plan, and suggest how these could be reduced or overcome.

Revision Guide pages 39, 40, 41, 42, 43, 44, 45, 46 and 60.

Hint

Many obstacles can be reduced or **overcome**. You must show how each obstacle can be tackled, so that Muhammad can meet his targets and achieve his goals. Be as **specific** and **detailed** as you can when making suggestions for overcoming barriers.

Hint

At the end of an assessment, read back through your answers, particularly the longer ones, to be sure they are accurate.

Hint

Make sure your answers show an ability to **select relevant information** from the scenarios and a good **breadth of knowledge**. For example, you could mention that some gyms are open 24 hours a day but these are often in towns, which might be far from Muhammad's village.

Hint

Try to make sure **all** your paragraphs are equally well written, each with an account of the obstacle **and** the method for minimising it.

Total for Question 6 = 8 marks

TOTAL FOR SECTION B = 30 MARKS TOTAL FOR TASK = 60 MARKS

Revision Guide pages 1, 5, 6, 9, 10, 12, 13, 16, 17 and 18.

Prepare

Use the information in this scenario to help you answer the assessment questions about Carl. Read carefully, **underlining** or **highlighting** any factors that affect his health and wellbeing.

Hint

To identify relevant factors, think about Carl's **PIES**: **P**hysical, **I**ntellectual, **E**motional and **S**ocial needs.

Prepare

Consider the likely effects on Carl's health of **smoking** from the age of 14. You should know about the short-term and long-term health risks of smoking.

Hint

Think about how working in a recycling plant and living in a town centre might affect Carl's health and wellbeing.

LEARN IT!

Pollution is contamination of the environment by chemicals, noise, heat and light.

Practice assessment 3

You must complete ALL questions.

SECTION A: Assessing health and wellbeing

You are a health care assistant at Orchard Road Medical Centre. You have been asked to assess the health and wellbeing of one of the service users.

Read the information below and then complete the activities that follow.

Location
Carl is 45 years old. He lives with his wife Paulette, aged 40, in a small terraced house with no garden, near the centre of a large town. They have a son, Ethan, who is 20 years old. He lives with his parents as he has moderate learning difficulties.

Medical history
Carl has a manual job, which keeps him active, but he gets out of breath more easily than he used to because he has smoked cigarettes since he was 14.

Family, friends and social interactions
Carl and Paulette have family and friends living close by. Although they don't manage to spend much time together during the week, at weekends they enjoy watching television and going to the local sports club for a pint of beer.

Day-to-day life
Carl works in a recycling plant and Paulette is a cleaner in a large factory. Their shift patterns mean that one of them is usually at home with Ethan while the other is at work. Carl eats junk food during the day and often enjoys a quick drink after work with his friends from the recycling plant. Paulette goes out to work in the evenings as soon as Carl gets home.

Your manager at Orchard Road Medical Centre has asked you to review the information about Carl.

1 (a) Explain **two social** factors that could have a **positive** effect on Carl's health and wellbeing.

Use the information provided.

1 ....

....

....

....

2 ....

....

....

....

4 marks

(b) Explain **one economic** factor that could have a **positive** effect on Carl's health and wellbeing.

Use the information provided.

....

....

....

....

2 marks

Revision Guide pages 1, 12, 16, 48, 50 and 51.

Hint

The word **review** tells you to assess information in the scenario in order to answer the questions.

Hint

For **explain** questions such as Questions 1(a) and 1(b), identify a point from the scenario about the named type of factor **and** expand on it. Back this up with your own knowledge.

LEARN IT!

Social integration is belonging to a group and interacting with other people.

Hint

Question 1(b) asks about **one economic** factor. Be sure to write about how Carl's **employment** and **financial resources** affect his health and wellbeing. Use words from the question to show that you understand what is being asked. For example, name an economic factor and say: 'This factor has a positive effect on Carl, because ...'

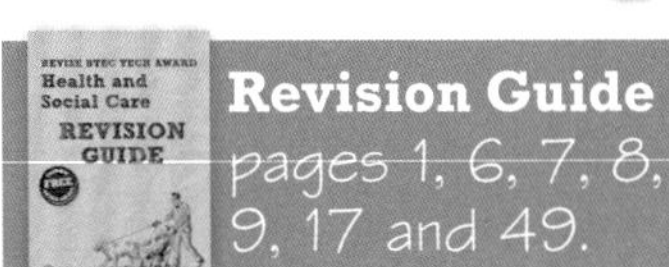

Revision Guide pages 1, 6, 7, 8, 9, 17 and 49.

Hint

Question 1(c) asks you to explain **two physical** factors from Carl's lifestyle that **negatively** affect him. If you use the same factor in a different way for the two answers, you will only be credited with the answer once.

Hint

Write neatly so that your answer is easy to read. If the assessor can't read your answer, they won't be able to mark it.

Hint

To do well at Question 1(d), first identify an **environmental** factor **and then** explain the negative effect it has on Carl's health and wellbeing.

Watch out!

As you are being asked to give examples of **negative** effects on Carl's health and wellbeing, you shouldn't include any positive effects.

(c) Explain **two physical** factors that could have a **negative** effect on Carl's health and wellbeing.

Use the information provided.

1 ....

....

....

....

2 ....

....

....

....

4 marks

(d) Explain **one environmental** factor that could have a **negative** effect on Carl's health and wellbeing.

....

....

....

....

2 marks

Total for Question 1 = 12 marks

Recently, Carl has been thinking a lot about his lifestyle and has decided that he wants to make some changes. He struggles with his reading and writing and is not very computer literate, but wants to be promoted to a more senior post at the recycling plant. His aim is to earn more money so that the family can move to a bigger house with a garden. Carl is aware that Ethan has been experimenting with cigarettes and alcohol with friends from the social support group he attends. Carl realises that he needs to change his own habits, so that he is a more positive role model for Ethan.

2 (a) Explain **two** effects that Ethan's learning difficulties could have on Carl's **emotional** wellbeing.

1 ....

....

....

....

2 ....

....

....

....

4 marks

(b) Explain **one** impact of Ethan's learning difficulties on Carl's **social** wellbeing.

....

....

....

....

2 marks

Total for Question 2 = 6 marks

Revision Guide
pages 1, 12, 13, 14, 30, 31, 49 and 51.

Prepare

Reread the scenario at the start of the assessment. Consider it along with the new information given here about Carl and Ethan.

Explore

A person with **moderate learning difficulties** like Ethan will struggle to acquire literacy, numeracy, problem-solving and communication skills. They may be less mature than their peers, find it harder to mix socially and may rely on adult support in their daily lives.

Hint

For Question 2(b), think about what a 20-year-old with no learning difficulties does on a daily basis. Compare this with what Ethan is likely to be doing. Think about how Ethan's additional needs could affect Carl's opportunities to **socialise** with family and friends.

Revision Guide
pages 6, 9, 10, 21, 24, 25, 26, 27, 52, 55 and 56.

Prepare

You should be familiar with the **physiological indicators**, such as BMI and peak flow, which are used to measure health.

Hint

You need to be able to interpret physiological data from charts, tables and graphs. To **interpret** the data about Carl's BMI, locate the row on the table where his BMI falls, and read off his weight category.

Hint

To **interpret** the data about Carl's peak flow, find his age on the horizontal axis. Follow the vertical line up from there until it meets the curve for men of his height. His expected peak flow is shown on the vertical axis level where the vertical line meets the curve. Compare with his actual peak flow.

Lifestyle data

Carl is worried about his increasing breathlessness so has made an appointment to see Dr Chang, his general practitioner (GP).

Dr Chang asks Carl some questions and records the following information:

- Carl smokes 40 cigarettes per day.
- Carl drinks alcohol almost every day.
- Carl eats junk food during the day.

Physiological data

Dr Chang records the following measurements.

Body mass index (BMI)	34.4 kg/m^2
Height	180 cm
Peak flow	482 l/min

Guidance for physiological data

Dr Chang gives this guidance to help you interpret the physiological data.

BMI

Weight categories	BMI (kg/m^2)
Underweight	<18.5
Healthy weight	18.5–24.9
Overweight	25–29.9
Obese	30–34.9
Severely obese	35–39.9
Morbidly obese	≥40

Peak flow

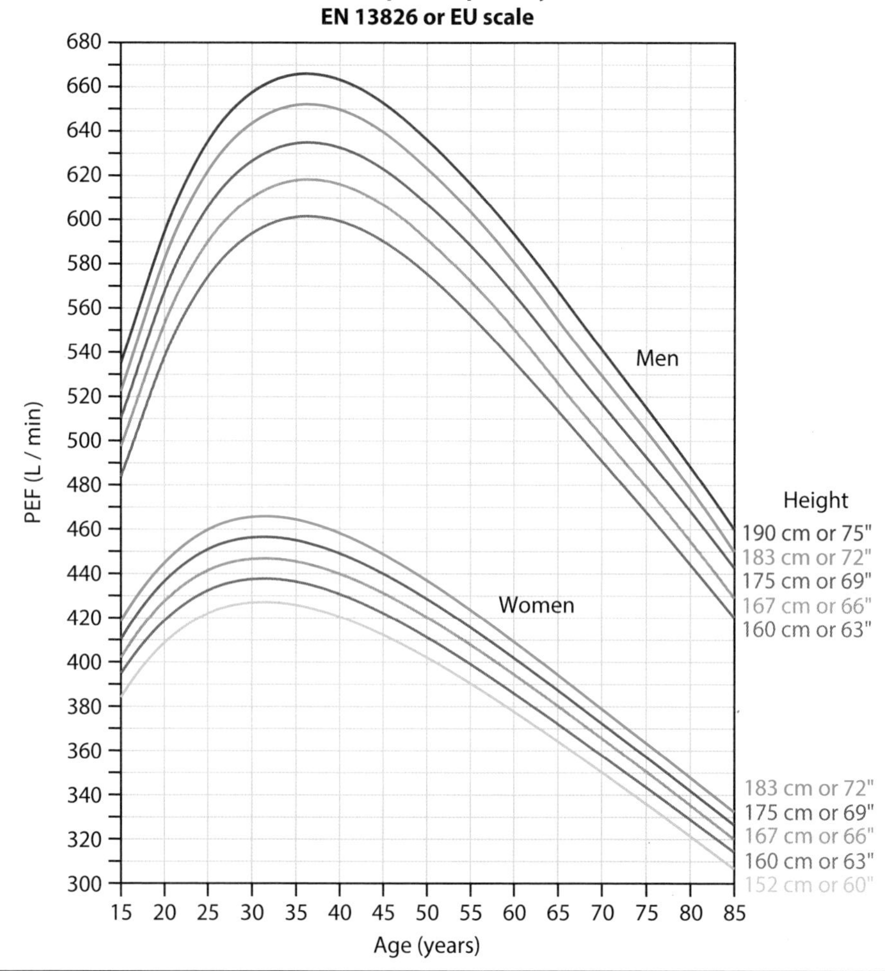

3 Explain what the data provided by Dr Chang suggest about:

- Carl's current physical health
- risks to his future physical health.

Lifestyle data	**Carl's current physical health:**
	....
	....
	....
	....
	Risks to Carl's future physical health:
	....
	....
	....
	....
BMI	**Carl's current physical health:**
	....
	....
	....
	....
	Risks to Carl's future physical health:
	....
	....
	....
	....

Revision Guide pages 52, 55 and 56.

Prepare

Look back at the information so far to find aspects of Carl's lifestyle that might affect his **BMI** and **peak flow**.

Hint

You need to interpret the data accurately, correctly identifying Carl's **BMI/ weight category** and **expected peak flow**. Then explain the **risks** to his **current** and **future** health if he continues his lifestyle. Do not make assumptions about lifestyle choices you have not been told about.

Hint

Be led by the total number of marks for the question and the writing space available. This question is split into three parts (lifestyle data, BMI and peak flow) and each of these is divided into current and future risks. Divide your effort equally between the six sections.

Hint

Smoking is one aspect of Carl's lifestyle that will affect his peak flow.

Hint

Read back through your answer to Question 3 to make sure it is legible, makes sense and includes all the information asked for.

Peak flow	**Carl's current physical health:**
	....
	....
	....
	....
	Risks to Carl's future physical health:
	....
	....
	....
	....

Total for Question 3 = 12 marks

TOTAL FOR SECTION A = 30 MARKS

SECTION B: Designing a health and wellbeing improvement plan

You have been asked to design a health and wellbeing improvement plan for Carl.

First you should look back at the information about Carl from Questions 1, 2 and 3.

Then study the notes below, taken by Dr Chang.

Carl wants to:

- stop smoking to improve his peak flow reading
- eat less junk food to eat more healthily and lose weight
- drink less alcohol.

Carl does not want to:

- totally stop drinking with his friends
- stop going to the sports club with Paulette at the weekends.

Other relevant information:

- Carl is motivated to improve his health to set a better example to Ethan.
- Carl is concerned about developing serious health issues later in life. He feels he needs to be there to look after Ethan in the future.
- Carl wants to be healthy, so that he is better prepared to take up new learning opportunities and improve his prospects.

Revision Guide pages 33 and 57.

Prepare

Review everything you have found out about Carl's lifestyle so far. Consider his **needs**, **wants** and **circumstances** shown here.

Hint

Your improvement plan should help Carl stop smoking, eat less junk food and cut his alcohol intake. Bear in mind that his **reading difficulties** could impact his ability to carry out your suggestions. Show that you understand his needs by considering ways to make your plan accessible to Carl.

Explore

Nicotine replacement therapy (NRT) supports smoking cessation by easing withdrawal symptoms such as cravings. It uses patches, inhalers, sprays or chewing gum to supply nicotine, the addictive substance in cigarettes, without the toxic chemicals in smoke. Not all types of NRT suit all people.

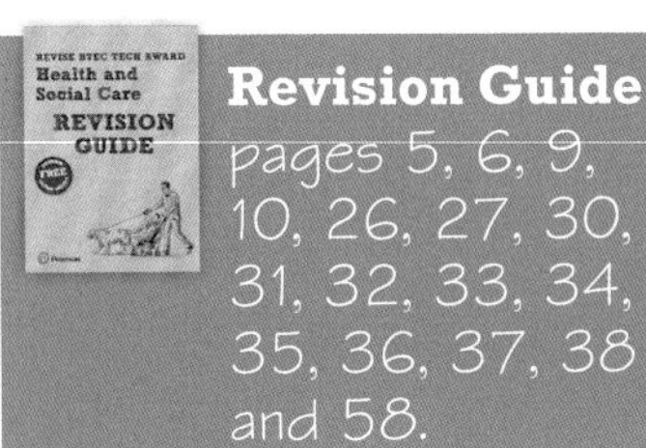

Revision Guide pages 5, 6, 9, 10, 26, 27, 30, 31, 32, 33, 34, 35, 36, 37, 38 and 58.

Hint

Key words used in Question 4: **design**, meaning to create or draw up a plan; **describe**, to give a clear account of each suggested action; **give**, to name a source of support; and **explain**, meaning to show how the support will help Carl.

Hint

A **recommended action** takes Carl's needs, wants and circumstances into account. For example, although Carl aims to cut his alcohol intake, he doesn't want to totally stop drinking.

Hint

A **realistic target** is sensible, suitable and achievable for Carl, given what you know about him from the scenario.

LEARN IT!

Short-term targets should be reached in the coming days and weeks, whereas **long-term targets** take more than six months to achieve, e.g. a year or maybe even two years, depending on what is right for Carl.

4 Design a health and wellbeing improvement plan for Carl. Your plan should describe **three** recommended actions.

For each recommended action:

- set a short-term and a long-term target
- give **one** source of support
- explain how the source of support will help Carl achieve the targets.

Recommended action 1
....
Short-term target
....
Long-term target
....
Source of support and how it will help
....

Recommended action 2

....

....

Short-term target

....

....

Long-term target

....

....

Source of support and how it will help

....

....

Recommended action 3

....

....

Short-term target

....

....

Long-term target

....

....

Source of support and how it will help

....

....

Total for Question 4 = 12 marks

Revision Guide
pages 6, 7, 10, 26, 28, 34, 35, 36, 37, 38, 43 and 58.

Hint

Refer to all the information you have learned about Carl in earlier parts of the assessment, to design the best health and wellbeing improvement plan for his situation. Include one action for each of Carl's different needs identified on page 34.

Hint

Make sure that your targets are clear, realistic and helpful by ensuring they are **SMART**: Specific, Measurable, Achievable, Realistic and Time-related.

Watch out!

You have to identify a source of support for each action **and** clearly state how it helps. The best sources of support for Carl will be **continuous** rather than one-offs, **reliable** and in place **in advance**.

Explore

Improvement plans should demonstrate the **seven care values** that underpin a **person-centred approach**: empowerment, dignity, respect, communication, anti-discriminatory practice, confidentiality and safeguarding.

Revision Guide
pages 29, 30, 31, 57 and 59.

Reread all of the information about Carl and his lifestyle throughout this assessment. You can demonstrate your depth of understanding by considering, for example, ways in which Carl could be a good role model for Ethan.

Before starting to write a longer answer, make a quick writing plan. Then, you should write out your answer in **full paragraphs**, taking care with spelling, punctuation and grammar. You could use the PEEL format: Make one Point, Explain this point, use Evidence to justify the point and explanation, and Link back to the question.

Hint

In order to explain your health and wellbeing improvement plan, write one paragraph for each action. Include a clear and detailed description of how each action relates to Carl's needs, wishes and circumstances. The best responses will include information about Carl from earlier in the scenario, to show good understanding about his health and wellbeing.

5 Explain how your health improvement plan takes into account Carl's needs, wishes and circumstances.

Total for Question 5 = 10 marks

Revision Guide pages 29, 30, 31, 57 and 59.

Hint

Read the question carefully **before** and **after** you answer. Check your response to be sure that you have answered the question properly.

LEARN IT!

Every paragraph should mention Carl's needs, wishes and circumstances:

A **need** is something Carl has to do to improve his physical, intellectual, emotional or social wellbeing.

A **wish** is a choice Carl can make, such as drinking with his workmates, so that the health and wellbeing improvement plan is easier for him.

A **circumstance** is an aspect of Carl's life, such as needing to get home after work to be with Ethan who has moderate learning difficulties.

Watch out!

A lot of space is provided for your answer, indicating that you are required to give a detailed justification of your improvement plan.

Revision Guide pages 39, 40, 41, 42, 43, 44, 45, 46 and 60.

Hint

The key word **describe** asks you to give a clear account of some possible **barriers** for Carl, linking these to information about him in the scenario. Then you should make realistic suggestions for overcoming them.

Hint

Write about at least three different obstacles, to show your breadth of knowledge.

Watch out!

This question asks about **possible** obstacles, so you have to think of problems that **could** happen, using your wider knowledge. For example, Carl's literacy problems could be an obstacle.

Hint

Effective support services are essential for success in overcoming obstacles. Be sure to give sufficient detail about **formal** and **informal** sources of support when making suggestions for overcoming barriers.

6 Describe possible obstacles that Carl may experience when trying to follow your health and wellbeing improvement plan, and suggest how these could be reduced or overcome.

Revision Guide pages 39, 40, 41, 42, 43, 44, 45, 46 and 60.

Hint

Health care professionals need to be able to explain obstacles that service users may face when following health improvement plans. They have to be able to communicate clearly, verbally and in writing. Check your answer to make sure your written language is clear and that you have used **correct spelling, punctuation** and **grammar**.

Hint

Don't leave questions unanswered. Try to think of something relevant to add. Use bullet points if you don't have time to write in full.

Hint

If you have time at the end, read over your answers and correct any mistakes. Neatly cross out any wrong answers.

Total for Question 6 = 8 marks

TOTAL FOR SECTION B = 30 MARKS **TOTAL FOR TASK = 60 MARKS**

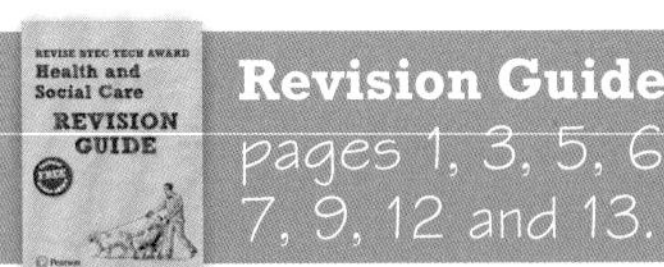

Revision Guide pages 1, 3, 5, 6, 7, 9, 12 and 13.

Use the information in the scenario to help you answer the questions about Yvonne in this assessment paper. **Underline** or **highlight** any factors that could affect Yvonne's health and wellbeing.

LEARN IT!

Arthritis is a chronic (long-term and incurable) illness. Movement is difficult due to pain, stiffness and swelling in the joints. Knuckles of the fingers, for example, may become deformed.

It is a great idea to practise answering assessment questions against the clock, so you are well prepared to work under **exam conditions**. You should be able to complete this paper in 2 hours.

The actual time allowed for your assessment could vary, so check with your tutor in advance.

Practice assessment 4

You must complete ALL questions.

SECTION A: Assessing health and wellbeing

You are a health care assistant at the Family Practice. You have been asked to assess the health and wellbeing of one of the service users.

Read the information below and then complete the activities that follow.

Location

Yvonne is 65 years old. She lives with her husband Martin, aged 70, in a bungalow surrounded by a garden, on the outskirts of a small town. There is a lane at the end of their road leading to walks across the fields. In the other direction and also within walking distance there is a large lake with footpaths and bird hides.

Medical history

Yvonne has been overweight since her early 20s. She is self-conscious about this but struggles to lose weight, turning to food for comfort whenever she is stressed or unhappy. She has arthritis in her joints. However, in her late 50s she had both knees replaced so her mobility is better than it has been for many years. Despite this, she can't kneel or take part in any high-impact exercise such as running. She wears a fitness tracker which monitors how far she walks each day, her heart rate and her sleep pattern.

Family, friends and social interactions

Yvonne and Martin have two children aged 31 and 32. Their son lives nearby, and they look after his children several times a week. Their daughter lives further away and they see their other grandchildren less frequently. They often eat out or go for drinks with family and friends, and each night before bed they enjoy a couple of glasses of whisky, which is their favourite alcoholic drink. They also holiday abroad several times a year, when they spend their time relaxing by the pool or sightseeing.

Day-to-day life

Yvonne and Martin are both retired teachers. They have good pensions, so do not struggle for money. Yvonne was an assistant headteacher in a high school when she retired and is now a school governor, which involves spending some time in school each week. She also gets paid to write school textbooks several times a year, sitting for long hours at her computer and often snacking while she types. When she has time and is not working on a book, she walks more.

Your manager at the Family Practice has asked you to review the information about Yvonne.

1 (a) Explain **two economic** factors that could have a **positive** effect on Yvonne's health and wellbeing.

Use the information provided.

1 ....

....

....

....

2 ....

....

....

....

4 marks

(b) Explain **one social** factor that could have a **positive** effect on Yvonne's health and wellbeing.

Use the information provided.

....

....

....

....

2 marks

Revision Guide pages 1, 12, 16, 48, 50 and 51.

Hint

The word **review** tells you to **assess** information in the scenario.

Hint

In Questions 1(a) and 1(b), **explain** questions, you need to identify points from the scenario about the particular type of factor and then give details to support your points.

Hint

Question 1(a) is about **two economic** factors. Give **two** ways in which the couple's **finances** (money) affect Yvonne's health and wellbeing.

Hint

Question 1(b) asks about **one social** factor, so write about Yvonne's chances to interact with other people. Do not write about any other type of factor.

Time it!

Look at the **mark allocation** for Section A and Section B and divide your time accordingly. Leave yourself a few minutes at the end to check over your answers.

Revision Guide
pages 1, 6, 7, 9, 49 and 51.

Hint

Question 1(c) asks you to explain **two** things that may give Yvonne negative feelings, such as being sad or worried. Identify the two factors and add some detail about each one to earn all the marks.

Watch out!

Questions 1(c) and 1(d) ask for examples of **negative** effects on Yvonne's health and wellbeing. No marks will be given for positive effects.

Time it!

Be sure to leave enough time to answer the longer questions at the end of the assessment. To be on track to complete the assessment in 120 minutes, you should spend a maximum of **24 minutes** doing Questions 1(a) to (d), including time to check your answers.

(c) Explain **two emotional** factors that could have a **negative** effect on Yvonne's health and wellbeing.

Use the information provided.

1 ....

....

....

....

2 ....

....

....

....

4 marks

(d) Explain **one physical** factor that could have a **negative** effect on Yvonne's health and wellbeing.

....

....

....

....

2 marks

Total for Question 1 = 12 marks

Martin has just been diagnosed with dementia, so is struggling to remember things, communication is becoming more difficult and he is exercising less. Until recently, Yvonne and Martin spent time doing word and number puzzles, attending a weekly pub quiz with friends. Martin has supported a football team since he was eight years old but is no longer able to attend games. However, increasingly, Yvonne is acting as his carer.

2 (a) Explain **two** effects that Martin's worsening dementia could have on Yvonne's **intellectual** wellbeing.

1 ....

....

....

....

2 ....

....

....

....

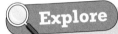

4 marks

(b) Explain **one** impact on Yvonne's **physical** wellbeing of having to look after Martin.

....

....

....

....

2 marks

Total for Question 2 = 6 marks

Revision Guide
pages 1, 3, 12, 14 and 20.

Prepare

Consider the scenario on page 44 and the information given there. Although you are told facts about Martin, remember that **Yvonne** is the focus of the assessment.

Explore

Dementia is a progressive (worsening) and eventually fatal decline in brain function. People experience memory problems, confusion, poor concentration, personality changes, social withdrawal, depression and loss of ability to do everyday tasks.

Hint

Don't forget in Question 2(b) that impacts can be **positive** or **negative effects**.

LEARN IT!

A healthy, active brain leads to **intellectual wellbeing**. This is an important aspect of a **holistic** (whole-person) approach to health and wellbeing.

Time it!

Don't spent too long on short-answer questions. You need time to develop your answers to the long-answer questions later in the assessment.

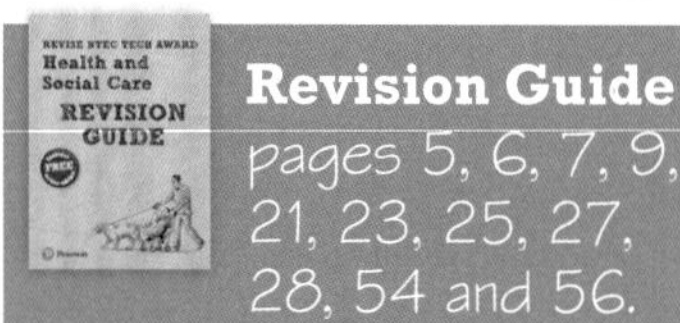

Revision Guide
pages 5, 6, 7, 9, 21, 23, 25, 27, 28, 54 and 56.

Prepare

You should be familiar with the **physiological indicators** such as **BMI** and **blood pressure** that are used to measure health.

Hint

Be sure to make links between the scenario and these pieces of data in your answer to Question 3.

Hint

To **interpret** Yvonne's BMI data, highlight the weight category in the table where her BMI falls.

Hint

To **interpret** Yvonne's blood pressure data, find the top number (140 mm Hg) on the vertical axis. Draw a line across from there. Find the bottom number (95 mm Hg) on the horizontal axis. Draw a line up from there. Note where the two lines cross and read off the blood pressure category.

Lifestyle data

Yvonne is worried about her weight so has made an appointment to see Dr Hilton, her general practitioner (GP).

Dr Hilton asks Yvonne some questions and records the following information:

- Yvonne eats too many snacks.
- She drinks alcohol every day.
- Yvonne finds it difficult to exercise as she has arthritis.

Physiological data

Dr Hilton records the following measurements:

Body mass index (BMI)	41.5 kg/m^2
Height	157 cm
Blood pressure	140/95 mm Hg

Guidance for physiological data

Dr Hilton gives this guidance to help you interpret the physiological data.

BMI

Weight categories	BMI (kg/m^2)
Underweight	<18.5
Healthy weight	18.5–24.9
Overweight	25–29.9
Obese	30–34.9
Severely obese	35–39.9
Morbidly obese	≥40

Blood pressure chart for adults

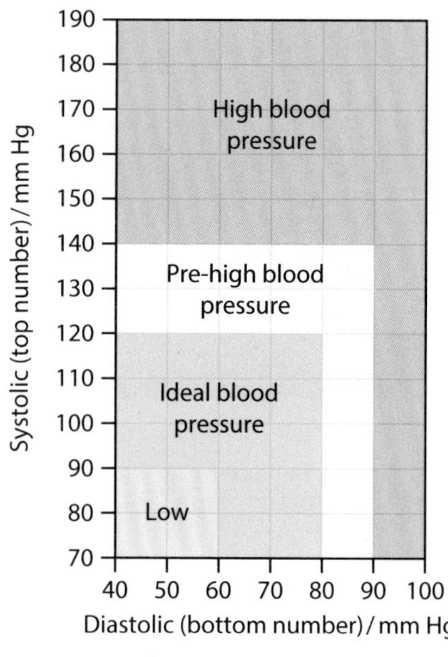

3 Explain what the data provided by Dr Hilton suggest about:

- Yvonne's current physical health
- risks to her future physical health.

Lifestyle data	**Yvonne's current physical health:**
	....
	Risks to Yvonne's future physical health:
	....
BMI	**Yvonne's current physical health:**
	....
	Risks to Yvonne's future physical health:
	....

Revision Guide pages 52, 54 and 56.

Hint

When interpreting lifestyle data, don't forget to reread all the information about Yvonne provided so far.

Prepare

Note down any information about Yvonne's lifestyle that might affect her **BMI** and **blood pressure**.

Hint

You need to interpret the data accurately, demonstrating this by correctly identifying Yvonne's **blood pressure** and **BMI/weight** categories. Then show that you know the implications for her **current** and **future** health.

Hint

When writing about risks to Yvonne's **future** health, use your **own knowledge** to describe what could happen if she continues her current lifestyle.

Time it!

Review how much time you have spent on Section A and check that you have enough time left for Section B.

Blood pressure	**Yvonne's current physical health:**
	....
	Risks to Yvonne's future physical health:
	....

Total for Question 3 = 12 marks

TOTAL FOR SECTION A = 30 MARKS

SECTION B: Designing a health and wellbeing improvement plan

You have been asked to design a health and wellbeing improvement plan for Yvonne.

First you should look back at the information about Yvonne from Questions 1, 2 and 3.

Then study the notes below, taken by Dr Hilton.

Yvonne wants to:

- exercise more to lose weight and keep her joints supple
- eat a more balanced diet to lose weight, help with her arthritis and improve her mental health
- drink less alcohol.

Yvonne does not want to:

- cut out all meals with family and friends
- totally stop drinking alcohol.

Other relevant information:

- Yvonne finds it hard to stick to a diet even though she knows it would improve her health and fitness.
- Yvonne is confident and outgoing but self-conscious about her weight.
- Yvonne wants to remain physically and emotionally fit and healthy, as she is caring for Martin.

Revision Guide pages 33 and 57.

Hint

Remember to keep in mind all the information about Yvonne's lifestyle so far when you read this new information.

Hint

Exercise could help Yvonne's **arthritis** and **fitness**.

Hint

Yvonne will be motivated to stick to your plan if she can **reduce**, not cut out, aspects of her lifestyle that she enjoys and finds relaxing.

Hint

Yvonne fills her retirement with lots of enjoyable activities. Your plan must fit into her unstructured days, whether she is writing a book, looking after grandchildren, caring for Martin, being a school governor or relaxing on holiday.

Explore

A diet rich in **omega 3 oils** and **vitamins** boosts emotional health and eases the symptoms of arthritis. For example, Yvonne could eat foods such as salmon, avocado, chia seeds, nuts and broccoli.

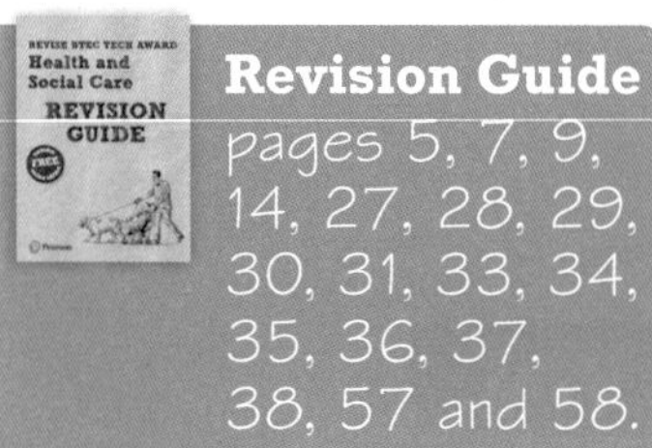

Revision Guide pages 5, 7, 9, 14, 27, 28, 29, 30, 31, 33, 34, 35, 36, 37, 38, 57 and 58.

Hint

The command word is **describe**. You need to give a clear account of each recommended action and link this to information about Yvonne from the scenario.

Hint

Use the **SMART** acronym to help make sure that your targets are realistic, specific and measurable:

Specific – clear and exact

Measurable – allowing Yvonne to track her progress

Achievable – possible for Yvonne

Realistic – suitable for Yvonne's needs and circumstances; and

Time-related – with a deadline.

Hint

The key word **give** asks you to name a source of support. You should also **explain** how the named support will help Yvonne.

Watch out!

The fourth line in each table asks for **two** pieces of information: a source of support **and** also how it will help Yvonne achieve the targets.

4 Design a health and wellbeing improvement plan for Yvonne. Your plan should describe **three** recommended actions.

For each recommended action:

- set a short-term and a long-term target
- give **one** source of support
- explain how the source of support will help Yvonne achieve the targets.

Recommended action 1 ....
Short-term target ....
Long-term target ....
Source of support and how it will help ....

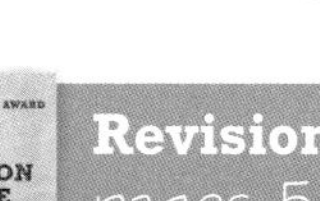

Recommended action 2

....

....

Short-term target

....

....

Long-term target

....

....

Source of support and how it will help

....

....

Recommended action 3

....

....

Short-term target

....

....

Long-term target

....

....

Source of support and how it will help

....

....

Total for Question 4 = 12 marks

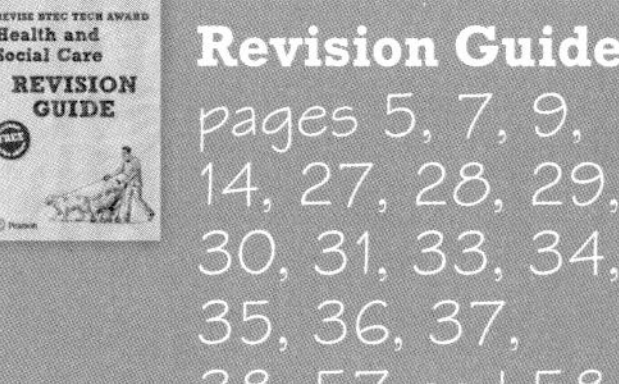

Revision Guide pages 5, 7, 9, 14, 27, 28, 29, 30, 31, 33, 34, 35, 36, 37, 38, 57 and 58.

Hint

Your **recommended actions** must improve Yvonne's health and wellbeing. They should be **person-centred**, with appropriate **short-term** and **long-term targets**.

Hint

Try to suggest sources that offer continuous rather than short-term support, as this will be more helpful to Yvonne.

Watch out!

Don't pick actions that are too similar. Include one action for each of Yvonne's different needs (more exercise, healthier diet and less alcohol).

Time it!

Question 4 is worth 12 marks. You should spend a maximum of **24 minutes** on it to be sure that you have time to complete the whole paper.

Revision Guide
pages 29, 30, 31, 57 and 59.

Prepare

Reread the information you have been given about Yvonne throughout this assessment paper. Use all the information to show **depth of understanding**.

Hint

As a health care professional, you would have to justify your plan to Yvonne. Write a paragraph explaining each recommended action. Include a comprehensive description of how each action takes into account her **needs**, **wishes** and **circumstances**, and show how this will empower her to follow your suggestions.

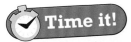

Time it!

It may be a good use of your time to make a **writing plan** for a longer answer.

5 Explain how your health improvement plan takes into account Yvonne's needs, wishes and circumstances.

Revision Guide pages 29, 30, 31, 57 and 59.

Hint

Check your **spelling, punctuation and grammar.** Ensure that what you have written makes sense. The assessor will find it easier to understand your answer if your writing is neat.

Watch out!

Try to use all the space that is available for this answer. The space tells you roughly how much information is expected.

Time it!

You should spend about **20 minutes** on Question 5. There is no writing frame, just lots of space. To keep your answer on target, check that every paragraph mentions Yvonne's **needs**, **wishes** and **circumstances.**

Time it!

You need to reserve about **16 minutes** to answer Question 6 and complete the assessment. If you have enough time left, quickly **check your Question 5 answer.**

Total for Question 5 = 10 marks

Revision Guide pages 39, 40, 41, 42, 43, 44, 45, 46 and 60.

Hint

Question 6 is a **describe** question. Give a clear and unbiased account of each **obstacle** (barrier), link each to information about Yvonne and make realistic suggestions for how to overcome the issues.

Prepare

Structure your answer with one paragraph for each obstacle. Use **PEEL** to plan each paragraph: make one **p**oint, **e**xplain it, use **e**vidence and **l**ink back to the question.

Hint

Show **breadth of knowledge** by describing a range of obstacles that are relevant to Yvonne, e.g. emotional barriers and time constraints.

Watch out!

Question 6 asks about **possible** obstacles, so you can include **your own knowledge** of obstacles to implementing improvement plans. However, your points **must** be relevant to Yvonne and her lifestyle.

6 Describe possible obstacles that Yvonne may experience when trying to follow your health and wellbeing improvement plan, and suggest how these could be reduced or overcome.

....

Total for Question 6 = 8 marks

TOTAL FOR SECTION B = 30 MARKS TOTAL FOR TASK = 60 MARKS

Hint

Consider whether your responses clearly **answer the questions**. Ask yourself whether your points are easy to understand, or whether they run into one another and become confused. If you need to clarify your answers, make some changes now.

Try to leave at least **five minutes spare to check over your paper**. Read through as many of your answers as possible and make changes if necessary. Neatly cross out any wrong answers. If you think of more information to improve your answers but are running out of time, add some bullet points.

Review how long it took you to complete the assessment. Think about how you could allocate your time differently to **improve your performance**.

Answers

Use this section to check your answers.
- For questions with clear correct answers, these are provided.
- For questions where individuals may give the correct answer phrased in different ways or there may be more than one correct answer, this is noted along with example answers.
- For questions that require longer answers, bullet points are provided to indicate key points you could include in your answer, or how your answer could be structured. **Your answer should be written using sentences and paragraphs** and might include some of these points but not necessarily all of them.

The questions and sample answers are provided to help you revise content and skills. Ask your tutor or check the Pearson website for the most up-to-date Sample Assessment Material, past papers and mark schemes to get an indication of the actual assessment and what this requires of you. Details of the actual assessment may change so always make sure you are up to date.

Practice assessment 1

(pages 1–14)

1 (a) Answers could include **two** from:
- Suzie has a garden; she gets exercise while digging the garden.
- Suzie exercises at the gym and lives in a three-storey house with lots of stairs; this helps her keep fit, giving her suppleness, stamina and strength.
- Suzie lives in a town; she is close to shops where she can buy healthy and fresh food.
- Suzie feels content and relaxed when gardening, and gains satisfaction and achievement from growing her own flowers.

(b) Answers could include **one** from:
- Suzie has a well-paid job as a teacher, so she has enough money to meet all her needs, such as a balanced diet, a comfortable home and plenty of clothes.
- Dave earns a high salary. Together with Suzie's income, they have no money worries; this gives Suzie peace of mind.

(c) Answers could include **two** from:
- Suzie has to bring planning and marking home with her, so she will not be able to socialise with family and friends during weekday evenings.
- Suzie works most evenings, so will not meet other people at the gym.
- Dave is often away overnight during the week so Suzie is on her own; she may feel socially isolated.

(d) Answers could include **one** from:
- Suzie worries about things and sometimes has panic attacks; this will make her unhappy and may cause low self-esteem.
- Suzie misses Dave during the week, so may feel miserable.
- When Suzie's weight goes up, she may feel embarrassed or unhappy and have low self-esteem.

2 (a) Answers could include **two** from:
- The accident was a serious shock, so Suzie may be upset.
- Dave's life was in danger through having sepsis; Suzie may have been very frightened.
- Suzie may feel unable to cope with Dave's accident and illness which could lead to low self-esteem.
- Dave will not be able to earn as much money while he is off sick; Suzie may be worried that they will get into financial difficulties.
- During his recovery, Dave will be at home; Suzie may be happy spending more time with him.
- Suzie may feel stronger through dealing with a challenging situation which could lead to higher self-esteem.
- Through supporting Dave, Suzie may feel closer to him, giving her emotional wellbeing a boost.

(b) Answers could include **one** from:
- Suzie may be tired from working full-time and looking after Dave in the evenings, so could feel less like socialising at weekends.
- Due to her caring responsibilities, Suzie will not be able to go to the gym, so will lose the opportunity to socialise with her friends there.
- Suzie is used to coming home to an empty house during the week; she may enjoy having Dave for company in the evenings.

3 Individual responses, for example:

Lifestyle data

Suzie's current physical health:
- Suzie eats an unhealthy diet, so is putting on weight.
- She binge drinks, which can cause increased blood pressure.
- She is finding it harder to exercise, so is putting on weight.

Risks to Suzie's future physical health:
- Suzie's unhealthy diet means she is more prone to illnesses such as diabetes, heart disease and stroke.
- Excessive alcohol intake over a long time causes damage to major organs (liver, heart, kidneys, pancreas and brain). It may also lead to depression and increases the risk of accidents due to poor judgement.

BMI

Suzie's current physical health:

Suzie's BMI of 29.3 puts her in the overweight category, close to being obese (30–34.9). Due to being so overweight, Suzie may experience these short-term issues:
- shortness of breath
- poor sleeping patterns
- raised blood pressure
- strain on her cardiovascular system.

Risks to Suzie's future physical health:

For Suzie, failing to lose weight in the long term means:
- reduced life expectancy due to cardiovascular disease and an increased risk of cancer
- high blood pressure and associated health risks, such as heart attack and stroke
- possible diabetes and associated health risks
- reduced mobility due to arthritis
- being increasingly less able to exercise, the larger she becomes
- potential poor self-esteem.

Blood pressure

Suzie's current physical health:
- Suzie's blood pressure of 160/95 mm Hg means she has high blood pressure.
- Suzie's has high blood pressure puts a strain on her cardiovascular system. As a result, she may feel a pounding or racing pulse and have headaches.

Risks to Suzie's future physical health:
- Long-term health risks of high blood pressure are stroke, heart disease, kidney disease and dementia.

4 Individual responses. Your answer should include **three recommended actions** that are described clearly, **each with**

one short-term and one long-term target. Targets should be specific and realistic. You must give a convincing explanation for how a source of support will help Suzie achieve the targets for each recommendation. Answers must be suitable for an overweight woman aged 25 years with high blood pressure.

There is a wide range of possible answers. Three examples of possible actions, with possible targets and support, are:

Recommended action 1: Do more exercise to lose weight and lower blood pressure.

Short-term target: Walk the 3 km distance to work and jog home.

Long-term target: Train over 20 weeks for a special event such as a 10 km run or a marathon.

Source of support and how it helps: Use a smartphone app or a training schedule to prepare for a run of a particular distance. Suzie is more likely to succeed if she uses a recognised training programme to build up gradually to a set distance.

Recommended action 2: Eat a balanced, healthy diet and cut down alcohol consumption to lose weight.

Short-term target: Make healthy choices, such as salads and no desserts when eating in restaurants, and alternate alcoholic drinks with water, low-alcohol drinks or diet soft drinks.

Long-term target: Learn to cook 10 new dishes that use fresh, healthy ingredients and cut out alcohol completely on weeknights.

Source of support and how it helps: Family and friends could support Suzie so that meals out take place in restaurants where there are healthy choices, and they do not persuade her to have alcoholic drinks.

Recommended action 3: Reduce stress to lessen worries and stop panic attacks.

Short-term target: Stay on at work after class to do marking and preparation, so that home becomes a work-free, stress-free environment.

Long-term target: Seek counselling for problems that cause panic attacks.

Source of support and how it helps: A counsellor would talk through issues with Suzie, to help her understand what causes her panic attacks. With professional help, Suzie would be able to address the causes, of the attacks and learn how to deal with them.

5 Individual responses. There are many possible answers, depending on what you wrote in your health and wellbeing improvement plan for Question 4. Your answer must accurately link the three actions you stated to what you know about Suzie's needs, wishes and circumstances from all the information provided about her lifestyle in the scenario. It is important that you write in full paragraphs.

Use one paragraph to **justify** each of the three actions, and **explain clearly and comprehensively** how that action takes into account **Suzie's needs, wishes and circumstances**. For example, here is a paragraph relating to Recommended action 2 from the suggested answer to Question 4:

*Suzie's **needs** are to reduce her BMI and blood pressure, and she **wants** to lose weight. A **recommended action** for Suzie is to eat a balanced, healthy diet to lose weight. A **short-term target** for Suzie is to ask friends to pick restaurants for their nights out which offer healthy options, such as grilled fish dishes and salads. A long-term target for Suzie is to learn to cook 10 healthy meals, which she may like to share with family and friends. These targets take into account Suzie's **wish** to socialise with family and friends during meals in restaurants, and also possibly at home when Suzie has perfected her new recipes. These targets take into account Suzie's **circumstances**, which are that she and Dave like to socialise with their family and friends over a meal at the weekend.*

Alternatively, you may wish to organise your answer by writing a paragraph on each of Suzie's **needs**, **wishes** and **circumstances**, showing how each of your three recommended actions take these aspects into account.

6 Individual responses. Your answer will be based on your own health and wellbeing improvement plan. You need to **clearly describe any obstacles** Suzie may face in trying to follow your plan and **make realistic suggestions for how these can be minimised**.

Examples of barriers and suggestions to minimise their impact could include:

- **Emotional/psychological barriers**. Suzie might eat snacks for comfort when tired, stressed or worried. She could overcome this by having healthy snacks, such as carrot batons and a low-fat dip, prepared in advance so she is not tempted to comfort eat.
- **Time constraints**. Suzie might find it hard to exercise in the evening because of her marking and planning commitments. She could overcome this by getting up 30 minutes earlier and doing a fitness DVD before work.
- **Availability of resources.** Suzie may not have access to any exercise equipment at home, but can overcome this by using, for example, cans of beans instead of weights when doing arm curls.
- **Unachievable targets**. A target of losing 5 kg in a week is unrealistic, but a target of losing 1 kg in a week is achievable.
- **Lack of support**. Suzie's friends might buy her usual alcoholic drink without asking her what she wants, putting temptation in her way. She should overcome this by telling her friends before they go out that she is cutting down her alcohol intake for health reasons and asking them to support her. This means asking what she would like to drink and not trying to persuade her to swap a non-alcoholic choice for an alcoholic drink.
- **Barriers to accessing services**. As Suzie is a teacher, she will only be able to access your recommended services out of school hours. Offer a choice of services so she can pick one that fits in with her work. For example, online or phone counselling might suit Suzie as she can fit it in around her work.
- **Other factors**. Suzie tends to worry about things, so she may worry about being able to follow your plan. This means you need to make your plan very clear, explaining the reasons for each suggested action and target.

Practice assessment 2

(pages 15–29)

1 (a) Answers could include **two** from:
- Muhammad has a big garden, so he can get fresh air and exercise, or relax outdoors.
- Muhammad has a luxurious house, so he will be comfortable and this may make him feel good.
- Muhammad lives in a village surrounded by countryside, so will be able to exercise by going for walks, or to relax in natural surroundings and feel calm.

(b) Answers could include **one** from:
- Muhammad has a large garden; he can do some exercise in the form of gardening.
- Muhammad has a large garden; he may feel a sense of satisfaction while gardening, and be relaxed and content.
- Muhammad lives in a village, so will be able to go for walks in the countryside and get some exercise in the fresh air.
- Muhammad plays golf which is good exercise and great for his mental health.

(c) Answers could include **two** from:
- Muhammad has a stressful job, so he may find it hard to switch off and relax in the evenings.
- Muhammad may worry about keeping up with his work demands, which will cause him stress.

- Muhammad may miss his children and grandchildren, as he only sees them in the school holidays.
- Muhammad is prone to chest infections. If he cannot see his children and grandchildren due to illness, he may feel guilty about not fulfilling his role as father and grandfather.

(d) Answers could include **one** from:

- Muhammad will be unhappy about the online abuse regarding his Muslim faith.
- Muhammad may not be able to pray when he is ill with a chest infection, so his cultural needs will not be met.
- Muhammad lives a long way from the nearest mosque so he cannot take part in a faith community; he may have low self-esteem if he feels he is not being a good Muslim.

2 (a) Individual answers. Answers could include **two** from:

Muhammad may feel lonely, as:

- he and Aamal can't continue their normal social life due to Aamal's stroke
- he has less opportunity to meet friends and play golf due to his caring responsibilities
- he and Aamal may be unable to travel to visit their family
- he may not be able to socialise at work as his working day is cut short by taking Aamal to her hospital appointments.

(b) Individual answers. Answers could include **one** from:

Muhammad may:

- feel reassured that Aamal is being cared for
- feel guilty that he is unable to care for Aamal full-time
- be worried that a male carer could be sent to help Aamal, which may not suit their cultural preferences
- be angry if their prayer routine is disrupted by carers who do not understand their culture
- be anxious that there are strangers in his house when he is not there to supervise them.

3 Individual responses, for example:

Lifestyle data

Muhammad's current physical health:

- Muhammad eats an unhealthy diet so may be putting on weight.
- He has frequent chest infections, so will find it hard to keep to an exercise regime, losing stamina, suppleness, strength and flexibility, and putting on weight.
- There is strain on his respiratory system due to his smoking, which makes him more prone to chest infections.

Risks to Muhammad's future physical health:

- If Muhammad continues to smoke, he could develop a smoker's cough and be at risk of emphysema, chronic bronchitis and lung cancer.
- If Muhammad doesn't change his diet, he will be less and less able to exercise and will be more at risk from diabetes, heart disease, cancers and stroke.

Blood pressure

Muhammad's current physical health:

- Muhammad's blood pressure of 170/100 mm Hg means he has high blood pressure.
- Muhammad's high blood pressure puts strain on his cardiovascular system. He may experience fluttering feelings in his chest and also headaches.

Risks to future physical health:

- Long-term health risks of high blood pressure are reduced life expectancy due to stroke, heart disease, kidney disease and dementia.

Peak flow

Muhammad's current physical health:

- Muhammad has low peak flow of 466 litres/minute, whereas a normal reading for a man of his age (55) and height (190 cm) is 630 litres/minute.
- He will be short of breath, especially while exerting himself, and may have sleep disruption.

Risks to Muhammad's future physical health:

- The risks to Muhammad's future physical health are from continued smoking, as described above.

4 Individual responses. Your answer should include **three recommended actions** that are described clearly, **each with one short-term and one long-term target**. Targets should be specific and realistic. You must give a convincing explanation for how a source of support will help Muhammad achieve the targets for each recommendation. Answers must be suitable for a male smoker, aged 55 years, with high blood pressure and caring responsibilities.

Three examples of possible actions, with possible targets and support:

Recommended action 1: Get more exercise.

Short-term target: Go for a brisk 30-minute walk around the village after dinner each night.

Long-term target: Jog instead of walk on three evenings each week.

Source of support and how it helps: Ask one of Aamal's friends to visit her each evening for 30 minutes, to allow Muhammad to go for his regular walk.

Recommended action 2: Eat a more balanced diet.

Short-term target: Shop online for healthier foods, so that Muhammad is not tempted to buy treats when in a store, and make better choices when eating out.

Long-term target: Eat at least 50 per cent vegetarian meals.

Source of support and how it helps: Use online vegetarian recipes and cookbooks with easy-to-follow recipes; this will allow Muhammad to eat more healthily for weight loss.

Recommended action 3: Stop smoking.

Short-term target: Reduce from 40 cigarettes a day to 30 in the first week and then reduce by another 5 each week.

Long-term target: Give up smoking completely after six months.

Sources of support and how it helps: A practice nurse can advise about smoking cessation and the use of nicotine patches, gum or lozenges to reduce cravings.

5 Individual responses. There are many possible answers, depending on what you wrote in your health and wellbeing improvement plan for Question 4. Your answer must accurately link the three actions you stated to what you know about Muhammad's needs, wishes and circumstances from all the information provided about his lifestyle in the scenario. It is important that you write in full paragraphs.

Use one paragraph to **justify** each of the three actions, and **explain clearly and comprehensively** how that action takes into account **Muhammad's needs, wishes and circumstances**. For example, here is a plan for a paragraph relating to Recommended action 1 from the suggested answer to Question 4:

- *One of Muhammad's needs is to get more exercise.*
- *A recommended action is to play golf at least twice a week.*
- *The plan includes asking a friend to visit Aamal while he plays golf. Alternatively, she could go with him in her wheelchair and socialise at the clubhouse while he plays.*
- *This action takes into account Muhammad's wish to continue playing golf.*

- *It also takes in account his circumstances, which are that someone needs to provide company and care for Aamal while he is playing golf.*

Alternatively, you may wish to organise your answer by writing a paragraph on each of Muhammad's **needs**, **wishes** and **circumstances**, showing how each of your three recommended actions take these aspects into account.

6 Individual responses. Your answer will be based on your own health and wellbeing improvement plan. You need to **clearly describe any obstacles** Muhammad may face in trying to follow your plan, and **make realistic suggestions for how these can be minimised**.

Examples of barriers and suggestions to minimise their impact could include:

- **Time constraints**. Muhammad might find it hard to exercise in the evening as he is looking after Aamal. He could go for a brisk walk in his lunch hour instead.
- **Availability of resources**. Muhammad may not have access to the right foods for a balanced diet as he has no time to shop. He could order ingredients online.
- **Unachievable targets**. For Muhammad, to give up smoking completely and immediately might be impossible. Instead, he may be more successful reducing gradually, so that he slowly gets used to less and less nicotine.
- **Lack of support**. If Muhammad joins his friends in the company smoking shelter (if there is one), they might offer him cigarettes. During breaks, he could go for a walk round the block with a non-smoking friend to distract him from cravings.
- **Barriers to accessing services**. Muhammad will only be able to access recommended services, such as a gym, outside work hours. He could find a gym that has opening times to suit his working hours and caring responsibilities.
- **Emotional/psychological barriers**. Muhammad might smoke for comfort when he is worried about Aamal or stressed about work. He could have healthy snacks to eat when he gets the urge to smoke, use NRT to reduce cravings or use electronic cigarettes to give him the familiar sensations of holding and sucking on a cigarette.
- **Other factors**.
  - o Muhammad may have difficulty fitting Aamal's hospital appointments around his usual working hours. He could talk to his boss to see if he can work flexible hours.
  - o Muhammad feels guilty about Aamal's stroke. He could see a counsellor to help him understand that it was her choice to work so hard and that the stroke would have happened anyway.

Practice assessment 3

(pages 30–43)

1 (a) Answers could include **two** from:

- Carl works, eats, smokes and drinks with his workmates every day during the week, so will enjoy their company, banter and being part of a group.
- Carl enjoys going to the sports club for a drink at the weekend where he can spend time with Paulette.
- Carl can spend time with Ethan when he gets home from work; they can talk about their day and do things together.
- Carl has family and friends living nearby, so is unlikely to feel socially isolated.
- Carl lives in the centre of a large town, so there are lots of opportunities to socialise.

(b) Answers could include **one** from:

- Carl has a steady job, so is likely to earn enough money to help meet their needs.
- Both Paulette and Carl work. Between them they should have enough money to meet their basic needs, so Carl will not be worried about money.
- Carl and Paulette earn enough to provide for Ethan who is not able to provide for himself.

(c) Answers could include **two** from:

- Carl smokes and has been doing so since he was 14; this is already causing shortness of breath and is likely to lead to other health problems.
- Carl eats junk food during the working day. This may lead to obesity and other conditions such as type 2 diabetes.
- Carl drinks alcohol most days. This may lead to obesity and other conditions such as high blood pressure or liver and heart disease.
- Carl has a manual job; he will sweat, which could lead to body odour and infections.

(d) Answers could include **one** from:

- Carl works in a recycling plant which could mean that he is exposed to dust and noise pollution.
- Carl works in a recycling plant; he could be exposed to dirt and germs, which could lead to a range of infections.
- Carl lives near the centre of a large town, so will be exposed to vehicle-exhaust pollution in the atmosphere. This can cause asthma and lung damage.
- Carl lives in a small terraced house with two others; it may be cluttered, which would make him more at risk of household accidents.
- Carl's house has no garden, so he will only be able to sit out in the fresh air if he walks to a park.

2 (a) Individual answers. Answers could include **two** from:

- Carl may feel anxious about how they will cope financially as Ethan is unable to work due to his learning difficulties.
- Carl may worry about how Ethan will cope with adult life, especially when he and Paulette are no longer around to look after him.
- If Carl can improve his literacy and his chances of promotion at work (which he wants to do so that he can look after Ethan better), his emotional wellbeing will improve, and he will be happier.
- Carl may feel anxious about the reactions of other people to Ethan when they are out and about.

(b) Individual answers. Answers could include **one** from:

- Carl has to rush home from his after-work socialising so that Paulette can go to work and he is home with Ethan.
- Carl may feel he cannot go out and leave Ethan in the house on his own, so this may limit his opportunities for social interaction in the evenings once Paulette has gone to work.
- Carl may feel that he and Paulette need to take Ethan with them when they go to the social club at the weekend, so he will be spending less quality time with his wife.
- Carl may be worried about setting a bad example for Ethan if they take him to the social club, so he may drink less to set a good example which could spoil the social occasion for him.
- Carl may enjoy spending his evenings and weekends with Ethan, giving him a feeling of contentment.

3 Individual responses, for example:

Lifestyle data

Carl's current physical health:

- Carl smokes 40 cigarettes a day and is breathless. He may have a smoker's cough and cravings for cigarettes. He may also have raised blood pressure.
- He drinks alcohol every day, so may put on weight, have mood swings and disrupted sleep patterns, and is at a greater risk of accidents.

- He eats junk food so may put on weight and feel less energetic. There could be a strain on his cardiovascular system due to excess weight.

Risks to Carl's future physical health:

- Carl will be less and less able to exercise.
- Obesity has a risk of cancer, heart disease, diabetes, stroke and arthritis.
- Carl is at risk of liver disease if he continues to drink alcohol every day.
- Long-term exposure to cigarette smoke causes emphysema and lung cancer.

BMI

Carl's current physical health:

- Carl's BMI of 34.4 kg/m^2 puts him in the obese category, close to being severely obese.
- He has shortness of breath, which may reduce his mobility.
- He may have raised blood pressure due to being obese.

Risks to Carl's future physical health:

- He will be prone to cancers due to obesity.
- Obesity also has a risk of heart disease, diabetes, stroke and arthritis.

Peak flow

Carl's current physical health:

- His peak flow reading of 482 l/min is lower than expected for a man of his age and height. (His reading should be 596 l/min.)
- Low peak flow is associated with breathlessness, lack of energy, tiredness and exhaustion.
- It is also an indication of possible lung problems, such as asthma and chronic bronchitis.

Risks to Carl's future physical health:

- He will be prone to lung cancers due to smoking.
- Long-term exposure to cigarette smoke causes emphysema.

4 Individual responses. Your answer should include **three recommended actions** that are described clearly, **each with one short-term and one long-term target**. Targets should be specific and realistic. You must give a convincing explanation for how each of your sources of support will help Carl achieve the target. Answers must be suitable for an obese and breathless 45-year-old who struggles with literacy.

There is a wide range of possible answers. Three examples of possible actions, with possible targets and support, are:

Recommended action 1: Stop smoking to improve peak flow reading.

Short-term target: Work out how much money Carl could save by cutting back his smoking and eventually stopping.

Long-term target: Stop smoking completely.

Sources of support and how it helps: Use a peak flow meter from the GP to monitor peak flow readings at home, and gain encouragement from seeing improvements.

Recommended action 2: Eat more healthily and lose weight.

Short-term target: Take a healthy packed lunch to work instead of buying junk food.

Long-term target: Have a healthier weight and so reduce BMI.

Source of support and how it helps: Ask workmates for support, so that they don't tease him or pressurise him to join them when they buy junk food.

Recommended action 3: Drink less alcohol.

Short-term target: Try low-alcohol or alcohol-free beer.

Long-term target: Stop drinking alcohol during the week, only drink in moderation when out at the weekend and never exceed the safe alcohol limit of 14 units spread over 3 or more days.

Source of support and how it helps: Ask Paulette to cut down too, so she can encourage Carl. In this way, both parents will set a better example to Ethan and become healthier. Carl's friends could also encourage him.

5 Individual responses. There are many possible answers, depending on what you wrote in your health and wellbeing improvement plan for Question 4. Your answer must accurately link the three actions you stated to what you know about Carl's needs, wishes and circumstances from all the information provided about his lifestyle in the scenario. It is important that you write in full paragraphs.

Use one paragraph to **justify** each of the three actions, and **explain clearly and comprehensively** how that action takes into account **Carl's needs, wishes and circumstances**. For example, here is a writing plan for a paragraph relating to Recommended action 3 from the suggested answer to Question 4:

- *One of Carl's needs is to drink less alcohol.*
- *A suggested action is to ask friends to support Carl by buying him a low-alcohol or soft drink unless he says otherwise when going out after work.*
- *This takes into account Carl's wishes to enjoy having a drink with his work mates.*
- *This also takes in account his circumstances, which are that Carl wants to set a better example to Ethan. He won't be coming home smelling strongly of alcohol.*

Alternatively, you may wish to organise your answer by writing a paragraph on each of Carl's needs, wishes and circumstances, showing how each of your three recommended actions take these aspects into account.

6 Individual responses. Your answer will be based on your own health and wellbeing improvement plan. You need to **clearly describe any obstacles** Carl may face in trying to follow your plan, and **make realistic suggestions for how these can be minimised**.

Examples of barriers and suggestions to minimise their impact could include:

- **Emotional/psychological**. Carl might turn to cigarettes for comfort, for example if he has a bad day at work. He could carry only the number of cigarettes allocated on the improvement plan for that day, and tell his workmates not to offer any.
- **Time constraints**. Carl might find it hard to remember to monitor and record peak flow readings when rushing to work in the morning. To make this a part of his daily routine, he could position the meter and chart next to his toothbrush or near the shower.
- **Availability of resources**. Carl could run out of aids such as NRT. He could set a reminder on his phone to go off several days before his supply runs out, so that he can stock up again.
- **Unachievable targets**. Totally giving up alcohol is not what Carl wants and may be unrealistic for him. It may suit him better to cut back gradually.
- **Lack of support**. Carl's friends may buy him junk food when they buy their own. He needs to tell them that he is serious about cutting down, and ask them to support and encourage him.
- **Barriers to accessing services**. Carl may be unable to access some of the information he needs because of his poor literacy skills. Provide the plan and supporting information in a format that suits him (audio or video resources may be useful) or ask Paulette to help him read the information.
- **Other factors**. Carl may try to make too many changes all at once, find it too much and succumb to temptation. This would make him feel guilty. He needs to understand that he will fail from time to time, that this is to be expected. He should just put it behind him and continue the plan the next day.

Practice assessment 4

(pages 44–57)

1 (a) Answers could include:
- Yvonne and Martin both have good pensions and do not struggle for money, so Yvonne can afford to meet all her needs, for example:
  - o physical needs (a balanced diet, nice clothes, a warm and comfortable house)
  - o intellectual needs (travel, puzzles and quizzes, other learning opportunities)
  - o emotional needs (content that she can afford her lifestyle)
  - o social needs (opportunities to interact with other people, such as meals out).
- Yvonne earns extra money by writing school textbooks, which helps her afford to meet her needs as above.

(b) Answers could include **one** from:
- Yvonne lives close to some of her family, so can enjoy their company often.
- Yvonne often eats out with family and friends, so has plenty of opportunity to socialise with others. This makes her happy and ensures that she is not bored or lonely in her retirement.
- Yvonne holidays abroad several times a year, so has many opportunities to spend time with Martin and interact with other holidaymakers.
- Yvonne is a school governor, so mixes professionally with adults and children at school. This gives her opportunities to interact with others and gain respect for her role.

(c) Answers could include **two** from:
- Yvonne may worry about her health and appearance as she is overweight.
- Yvonne may feel a failure and have low self-esteem as she is unable to control her weight.
- Yvonne may be miserable with pain from arthritis, and she may dislike how her joints look.
- Yvonne may be frustrated by her lack of mobility; for example, not being able to kneel to garden or do any high impact exercise to help her lose weight.
- Yvonne may feel guilty that she helps her son with his children more than she helps her daughter.
- She may feel sad that she doesn't see her daughter and her daughter's children as often as she sees her son and his children.

(d) Answers could include **one** from:
- Yvonne's weight means she is likely to be less fit and is at risk of diseases associated with obesity, such as type 2 diabetes, heart disease, stroke and cancer.
- Yvonne's arthritis means that she may not be as fit as she could be for her age. She could have reduced mobility and reduced bone density, and be unable to do certain exercises which would help maintain her suppleness, stamina and strength.
- Yvonne drinks alcohol every day, increasing her risk of depression, liver disease and certain cancers.

2 (a) Individual answers. Answers could include **two** from:
- Yvonne will be tired from looking after Martin, so may be less able to concentrate on her textbook writing.
- Yvonne will be worried about Martin, so could be distracted from her work as a school governor.
- Yvonne may have to give up her writing work and position as a school governor as Martin's condition worsens and she needs to look after him. This will limit the opportunities to keep her brain active.
- Yvonne and Martin will be less able to travel as his dementia progresses, limiting Yvonne's opportunities to discover new places and stimulate her brain.
- Yvonne and Martin will be less able to do puzzles together as his condition worsens, limiting Yvonne's opportunities to stimulate her brain.
- Yvonne will be less able to attend the weekly pub quiz as Martin's condition progresses, because she may need to be at home looking after him instead. This will limit her opportunities to keep her brain active.

(b) Individual answers. Answers could include **one** from:
- Yvonne may have fewer opportunities to go out for a walk as Martin's condition worsens, so she will be less fit.
- Yvonne might walk more if she and Martin walked together. It is helpful for people who live with dementia to walk, and this could have a positive impact on her physical health and wellbeing.
- Yvonne may have less time to prepare healthy meals as she has to devote more time to keeping Martin safe, so she may put on weight.
- Yvonne will spend more time at Martin's medical appointments and waiting in for various healthcare services for him. She will have less time to keep fit by gardening or walking.
- Yvonne will be sad as she feels she is losing Martin through dementia and may turn to food and alcohol for comfort. She might struggle even more with her weight and arthritis, increasing the risks to her future health.
- Yvonne may decide to devote herself to looking after Martin, preparing healthy meals for them both and making sure they go out for a walk together while they still can. This would initially have a positive impact on her.
- Yvonne may get less sleep as she needs to support Martin more with his personal care. This could lead to her becoming exhausted, and her resistance to infection may be reduced.
- She may develop musculoskeletal problems through moving and handling when she cares for Martin.

3 Individual responses, for example:

Lifestyle data

Yvonne's current physical health:
- Yvonne eats too many snacks so could be putting on weight.
- She drinks alcohol every day, so could be putting on weight and may have mood swings and disrupted sleep patterns. She may also be at a greater risk of accidents.
- Yvonne will find it harder to exercise due to her arthritis and weight, so will lose stamina, suppleness, strength and flexibility, and will also put on more weight.
- There will be a strain on Yvonne's cardiovascular system due to excess weight.

Risks to Yvonne's future physical health:
- If Yvonne doesn't change her lifestyle, she will be at risk of cancers, heart disease, diabetes and stroke due to her obesity. Her arthritis might also get worse if she continues to gain weight.
- She is at risk of liver disease if she continues to drink alcohol every day.

BMI

Yvonne's current physical health:
- With a BMI of 41.5 kg/m^2, Yvonne is in the morbidly obese category.
- She is likely to have shortness of breath and reduced mobility.
- She could have raised blood pressure due to the strain on her cardiovascular system.

Risks to Yvonne's future physical health:

- She will be at risk of cancers, heart disease, diabetes and stroke due to her obesity. Her arthritis might also get worse as her weight will place a strain on her joints.

Blood pressure

Yvonne's current physical health:

- Yvonne's blood pressure reading of 140/95 mm Hg means she has high blood pressure.
- Due to high blood pressure, Yvonne could experience headaches, vision problems, confusion and fatigue.
- Due to the strain on her cardiovascular system, she may have an irregular heartbeat and pounding in her chest and ears. She could even have chest pains and shortness of breath.

Risks to Yvonne's future physical health:

- Yvonne's high blood pressure could mean she has a reduced life expectancy as she is at risk of stroke and coronary heart disease.

4 Individual responses. Your answer should include **three recommended actions** that are described clearly, each with **one short-term and one long-term target**. Targets should be specific and realistic.

You must give a convincing explanation for how each of your sources of support will help Yvonne achieve the target. Answers must be suitable for a morbidly obese 65-year-old with arthritic joints and knee replacements.

There is a wide range of possible answers. Three examples of possible actions, with possible targets and support, are:

Recommended action 1: Get more exercise.

Short-term target: Move about more: get up and walk around for 5 minutes every hour when working at the computer, and go for a 30-minute walk every day with Martin. (This action would benefit Martin's physical and mental health as well as Yvonne's, and would mean that Yvonne could continue to supervise him while also taking exercise.)

Long-term target: Aim to walk 10,000 steps every day, more briskly as Yvonne gets fitter.

Source of support and how it helps: Yvonne has a fitness tracker. She will be motivated to continue this action as the tracker records more steps or increasing distances walked in 30 minutes and a healthier heart rate. It could be set to alert her if her activity levels drop.

Recommended action 2: Eat a more balanced diet to lose weight, help with arthritis and improve Yvonne's mental health.

Short-term target: Plan rewards for stages in weight loss, for example, every 2 kg, as an incentive. Treats could include anything that Yvonne would find motivating, such as a puzzle book, a shopping trip with a friend or new handbag.

Long-term target: Maintain new healthy eating habits.

Source of support and how it helps: Join a slimming club for advice and motivation while a family member looks after Martin.

Recommended action 3: Drink less alcohol.

Short-term target: Start by cutting down to one glass of whisky each night.

Long-term target: Drink in moderation when out with friends, have an occasional whisky in the evening and never exceed the weekly recommended limit of 14 units spread over three days or more.

Source of support and how it helps: Encourage Martin to cut down too, so Yvonne doesn't feel she is missing out when he pours a whisky at night.

5 Individual responses. There are many possible answers, depending on what you wrote in your plan for Question 4. Your answer must accurately link the three actions you stated to what you know about Yvonne's needs, wishes and circumstances from all the information provided about her lifestyle in the scenario. It is important that you write in full paragraphs.

Use one paragraph to **justify** each of the three actions, and **explain clearly and comprehensively** how that action takes into account **Yvonne's needs, wishes and circumstances**. A plan for one paragraph might be:

- *One of Yvonne's needs is to eat a more balanced diet.*
- *One suggested action in your plan might be to attend a slimming club where her weight loss will be monitored and she will get advice on healthy eating and healthy menu choices when eating out. Yvonne will need family support to achieve this as someone will have to care for Martin while she is out.*
- *This action takes into account Yvonne's wish to continue going out for meals with family and friends.*
- *This action also takes into account Yvonne's circumstances, which are that Martin has dementia and needs someone to make sure he is safe, and that she needs to lose weight to be fit and healthy.*

6 Individual responses. Your answer will be based on your own plan. You need to **clearly describe any obstacles** Yvonne may face in trying to follow your plan, and **make realistic suggestions for how these can be minimised**.

Examples of obstacles and suggestions to minimise their impact could include:

- **Emotional/psychological barriers**. Yvonne might snack for comfort when worried about Martin or when stressed about fitting in her writing and school governor commitments with looking after him. She could have healthy snacks ready for occasions when she needs comfort food, instead of grabbing something unhealthy such as biscuits or crisps. She could also choose snack foods that benefit her emotional and physical health, such as nuts and seeds.
- **Time constraints**. Yvonne might find it hard to exercise because of the time it takes to look after Martin. They could go for a walk together or Yvonne could ask a family member to sit with Martin so that she can go for a walk or a swim.
- **Availability of resources**. Yvonne may not have access to a swimming pool if she is looking after Martin, so could use a low-impact exercise DVD instead.
- **Unachievable targets**. It might be difficult for Yvonne to lose 2 kg of weight a week, after the initial larger losses at the start of a diet. A more achievable target is 1 kg a week, with any extra weight loss as a bonus.
- **Lack of support**. Yvonne's friends may tempt her with alcoholic drinks, thinking that she needs them to relax when she is stressed about looking after Martin. She needs to explain to them that she is serious about cutting down and that she would like them to support and encourage her.
- **Barriers to accessing services**. Yvonne may find she cannot get to her slimming club meetings if Martin's condition worsens. She needs to plan ahead to make sure that family and friends are available to help with Martin so she can keep going to the club. Alternatively, she could use a diet app or an online support programme instead of going to meetings.
- **Other factors**.
  - o Yvonne may feel guilty going out and having fun with friends when Martin's condition is worsening. Her family and friends need to remind her that if she is happier and more relaxed after taking time for herself, she will be better able to look after Martin.
  - o Yvonne's arthritis and knee replacements may stop her from doing weight-bearing exercise. She could try aqua aerobics instead.

Notes

Notes

Notes

Notes